LESSONS *from* BABEL

DENNIS A. MCINTYRE

LESSONS FROM BABEL

Copyright © 2023 Dennis A. McIntyre

This is a work of fiction. All of the characters, names, incidents, organizations, and dialogue in this novel are either the products of the author's imagination or are used fictitiously.

Bennett books may be ordered through booksellers or by contacting:

Bennett Media and Marketing
1603 Capitol Ave., Suite 310 A233
Cheyenne, WY 82001
www.thebennettmediaandmarketing.com
Phone: 1-307-202-9292

ISBN: 978-1-957114-79-8 (Paperback)
ISBN: 978-1-957114-80-4 (eBook)

Printed in the United States of America

FOREWORD

At the age of 25 I accepted Christ as my personal savior. During my early Christian years, I found myself testing and often questioning Biblical accounts, the events leading up, what they meant then, and how I am to apply them today. This process has been an on-going one for me for over 30 years now. I am not saying that this was in any way a wrong approach, as I believe we are commanded to test the scriptures (1Thes.5:21). I have grown closer to my Lord and trust the process will continue until I am called away.

Most of the time I have understood what truths were to be gleaned from each account, but on occasion the complete answer was held from me. I would accept those times and move on. Yet, in the back of my mind was a wee voice still wondering about some accounts. This book is the result of revelations to at least two events that took place in Genesis that really impacted me as an early Christian. The following scripture is the basis for my studies:

The Tower of Babel (KJV) Gen.11:6

6. And the LORD said, Behold, the people *is* one, and they have all one language; and this they begin to do: and ***now nothing will be restrained from them, which they have imagined to do.***

The highlighted section struck a chord in me when I first read it as if to say that we have the power to do anything when we work together for a common purpose. The world today speaks many languages, but when everyone begins to speak one language again, our world can have a brighter future. The language of love is universal and needs to be spoken, especially by those who profess to follow Christ, who is love. I believe that we still have God-ordained power to accomplish much here on earth and that our only barrier is ourselves.

TABLE OF CONTENTS

INTRODUCTION

Where did we come from?

That's a question that has been asked throughout the ages. No one was around when life began, so we need to come to a personal conclusion. The choices are simple. Either we arrived by a series of random events that started with the simplest elements combining, and then over long periods of time evolved to where we are today, or we were created. If we evolved, then we have no sustaining purpose. When we die we die. Therefore, life is whatever we choose to make it while we are here.

If we were created, then several more questions may be asked like:
- Why? (For what purpose?)
- Is the creator still with us and if so can we communicate with him?
- Is this the end or is there life after we die?
- Are we being tested?

For those who believe that we are here by random chance, I admire your faith. To believe that there is no creator (god) is as much an act of faith as to believe that there is. Not one of us was there when this world was formed. Therefore, we would rely only on our own conclusions based on whatever evidence we see today. To believe there is no master plan with all of the evidence we see in nature alone takes enormous faith to be sure. Sir Fred Hoyle, made the following statement after studying the intricacies of the human eye. In referring to the possibility that an eye could reproduce itself by random chance would be like "a hurricane blowing through a junk yard and assembling a 747 on the other side. I do not share this faith.

> *'The chance that higher life forms might have emerged in this way is comparable with the chance that "a tornado sweeping through a junk-yard might assemble a Boeing 747 from the materials therein"'*[1]

After examining the evidence, I not only believe that there is a master creator, but I believe he is eternal. That brings about the next question: "Why am I here?" Each of us may already have asked that question. Since we are only alive on this earth for a short time, then another question comes to mind; "Do we have a purpose for being here?" If we choose to answer that, we must be here for a reason then we must find what it is. If not, then any future life after death experience would also be meaningless. If we live as though there is no purpose and we are wrong, then we will have failed. Therefore, I choose to seek what my purpose on earth is and live accordingly in case there is more to come.

Since we are all on this earth together, then it makes sense, at least to me, that we need to find ways to communicate with one another. You might come to the conclusion that we are gathered here for that purpose, so we will be better prepared for any life to come. In other words, one person does not have all the answers, but collectively we may be able to put the pieces together.

Since I believe in a creator, then I also believe that he is able to communicate with us, and that the Bible is his word. This account comes in the first nine verses of chapter 11 in the book of Genesis. Here we find a group of people building a city with a tall tower in the middle.

---

1   Sir Fred Hoyle (English astronomer, Professor of Astronomy at Cambridge University), as quoted in 'Hoyle on Evolution'. Nature, vol. 294, 12 November 1981, p. 105.

It was typical for towers to be built in those days so that inhabitants can climb high above the city to see if there are intruders approaching. This account tells us that the tower was to be more, much more than that. It was to be a symbol of pride for all to see.

In these nine verses we read about the motives of the people, their unity, the affect they had on the creator, and their ultimate demise. In the pages that follow, we will look deeper into the history behind Babel and try to uncover some deeper meanings that we can still apply today. Someone once said that the best predictor of future behavior is past behavior. Perhaps, the things that caused their downfall can be corrected by new behavior today. Let's take a look into the past. Perhaps we can learn something about the human spirit or find answers to questions that still linger in ours.

DENNIS A. MCINTYRE

THE BABEL ACCOUNT (GEN.11: 1-9)

The Tower of Babel (KJV)

1 And the whole earth was of one language, and of one speech.

2 And it came to pass, as they journeyed from the east, that they found a plain in the land of Shinar; and they dwelt there.

3 And they said one to another, Go to, let us make brick, and burn them throughly. And they had brick for stone, and slime had they for morter.

4 And they said, Go to, let us build us a city and a tower, whose top may reach unto heaven; and let us make us a name, lest we be scattered abroad upon the face of the whole earth.

5 And the LORD came down to see the city and the tower, which the children of men builded.

6 And the LORD said, Behold, the people is one, and they have all one language; and this they begin to do: and now nothing will be restrained from them, which they have imagined to do.

7 Go to, let us go down, and there confound their language, that they may not understand one another's speech.

8 So the LORD scattered them abroad from thence upon the face of all the earth: and they left off to build the city.

9 Therefore is the name of it called Babel; because the LORD did there confound the language of all the earth: and from thence did the LORD scatter them abroad upon the face of all the earth.

Let's look at the scripture in a little more detail verse by verse.

VERSE 1:
ONE LANGUAGE

1 And the whole earth was of one language, and of one speech.

Several generations have now passed since the Ark found dry ground on the Mount of Ararat, with Noah's sons moving across the known lands and establishing new families. Chapter 10 names several of the offspring for each of the sons. This traveling has moved each family farther and farther away to repopulate the earth. Yet, through everything, there was still only one language and a common speech (dialect). It might be an interesting study to see how many generations it would take to form separate and unique dialects today, when people separate and migrate to new locations. I for one can envision a very short time would pass before local slang started creeping into conversations as people seek to form new identities. In this account the point was made up front, that had not happened yet. Somehow, continuity was maintained despite the mass separation that had taken place. Everyone understood each other. They were in a single accord.

Genesis chapter 10 holds some key information about how the separation of languages at Babel affected the descendents of Japheth, Ham, and Shem. At the end of the account we see the words (vs 4,20, 31):

"by their clans and languages"

At Babel (Gen.11:1) we read that the world was with one language and one speech. The new world after the flood seems to have been given a common communication practice for the generations that followed up to this time. God desired a different result than before the flood.

Pentecost (Acts 2:1-11)

After Christ had conquered death at the cross, believers gathered in one place, each with their own language and dialect. The Holy Spirit filled them and they were able to hear the message from God in their own language simultaneously.

1 And when the day of Pentecost was fully come, they were all with one accord in one place.

2 And suddenly there came a sound from heaven as of a rushing mighty wind, and it filled all the house where they were sitting.

3 And there appeared unto them cloven tongues like as of fire, and it sat upon each of them.

4 And they were all filled with the Holy Ghost, and began to speak with other tongues, as the Spirit gave them utterance.

5 And there were dwelling at Jerusalem Jews, devout men, out of every nation under heaven.

6 Now when this was noised abroad, the multitude came together, and were confounded, because that every man heard them speak in his own language.

7 And they were all amazed and marvelled, saying one to another, Behold, are not all these which speak Galilaeans?

8 And how hear we every man in our own tongue, wherein we were born?

9 Parthians, and Medes, and Elamites, and the dwellers in Mesopotamia, and in Judaea, and Cappadocia, in Pontus, and Asia,

10 Phrygia, and Pamphylia, in Egypt, and in the parts of Libya about Cyrene, and strangers of Rome, Jews and proselytes,

11 Cretes and Arabians, we do hear them speak in our tongues the wonderful works of God.

I picture a radio station broadcasting all channels in unique languages, where each person was tuned in to the station they could understand. Once again they were unified. Observers thought that these believers were drunk as is recorded in the following verses of the chapter, but Peter is quick to respond that is was still morning (vs 15). It appears as though, when people are left to their own desires, God is left outside. At Pentecost they were anxiously awaiting God's presence and were not disappointed. Immediately afterwards, these people went out with great power performing many miracles through the Holy Spirit.

Questions to ponder:

How important is it to God today to have Christians all speaking the same language?

What language would that be?

What would the message include?

Are Christians speaking in one accord today?

VERSE 2:
NEW HOME

2 And it came to pass, as they journeyed from the east, that they found a plain in the land of Shinar; and they dwelt there.

This was the result of an easterly migration, where the people came upon a desirable plain where they can make their roots. The plain was called "Shinar", which has been translated "Babylonia". In Genesis Chapter 10 we read about the descendents of Ham settling there.

Ham's son Cush and grandson Nimrod:

Genesis 10:8-11 (KJV)

8 And Cush begat Nimrod; he began to be a mighty one in the earth.

9 He was a mighty hunter before the LORD: wherefore it is said, Even as Nimrod the mighty hunter before the LORD.

10 And the beginning of his kingdom was Babel, and Erech, and Accad, and Calneh, in the land of Shinar.

11 Out of that land went forth Asshur, and builded Nineveh, and the city Rehoboth, and Calah,

The study of the descendents of Ham will be an important topic discussed later. In any event these people were looking for a place to settle down and this was to be that place. The geographical location of Babylon is a fertile area near the Euphrates River in the modern country of Iraq (known as Mesopotamia). To reach this area from the west would be a rugged trek across desert. No wonder why it looked so inviting.

Why do people migrate today?

- Escape tyranny, oppression
- Better life (economically)
- Better climate
- New job

These people were leaving a place without hope to seek a place with it. We will address their sense of hopelessness later.

VERSE 3:
UNITY

3 And they said one to another, Go to, let us make brick, and burn them throughly. And they had brick for stone, and slime had they for morter.

The words "Go to" implies action. I do not claim to be a scholar on the King James language, but following a comma is a capital "G." Perhaps, this was their voice of unity. In one accord they desired to build a place to call home. They chose to do so using hand made bricks instead of stone, a valuable training that is later used by descendants in slavery in Egypt. This may have been the best choice due to the shortage of stone deposits in the area. These bricks would be held in place with tar to ensure strength. In any event they purposed to make this a well-designed (state of the art) undertaking. This implies that they were prideful in their intentions. On the surface that is a very good thing.

We have all heard of the three little pigs' story, where each one used different housing construction to create homes. When the big bad wolf came along, only the one made of brick stood strong. Perhaps, these people were of the mindset to go for the best up front. This may take a lot longer. But they were together in unity of purpose to achieve the best.

The act of baking bricks took a team effort. Straw needed to be chopped and mixed with clay. Then they formed them into molds to dry in the sun. These would have to be transported to the site, where the mortar would be added by another group of men. The process required diligence, patience, and most of all close supervision. In addition, there had to be a drainage system in place to prevent erosion. This system would require continuous cleaning to prevent back up. Earthquakes could shake the foundation without proper building techniques. This was a highly concentrated and unified effort. Each worker possessed different skills, which required monumental supervision with continual checks and balances. This was to be an architectural masterpiece.

Verse 4:
Pride

4 And they said, Go to, let us build us a city and a tower, whose top may reach unto heaven; and let us make us a name, lest we be scattered abroad upon the face of the whole earth.

Beyond the building of dwelling places in which they would live, they desired much more:

- They desired a city that anyone who approached would see greatness.
- They desired a monument (tower) that would reach into the heavens so everyone would truly be impressed.
- They desired recognition (a name for ourselves), so that they would receive accolades.
- They desired refuge so that they would never have to wander (be scattered) again.

Pride went beyond that, which we might have for our home or families. We will study more about their background later, but these people were looking for far more than they had before. They were hungry for recognition and tired of feeling like third class citizens.

Archaeologists have uncovered what appears to be a foundation of a tower approximately 300 feet square. An inscription made by King Nebuchadnezzar indicates the tower was rebuilt with brick enabled in brilliant blue. Like the Egyptian construction of the Great Pyramids, the tower would have gradually increased in height, while having the widest support at the base. This was no small undertaking. It would have been a modern wonder at that time. It certainly would have demanded respect from all who visited the city and viewed a long distance away. The people would also have to be totally committed to the project to complete it. In 460 BC a Greek historian by the name of Herodotus visited a deteriorated tower and was very impressed. He described it as having eight levels all square in shape. Running around the outside was a spiral stairway with many seats, where people were allowed to rest.

The walls would have been much larger totally surrounding the city. Walls were commonly constructed around cities in the day as protection. All of this would have been a monumental undertaking to be sure.

VERSE 5:
THE LORD'S VISIT

5 And the LORD came down to see the city and the tower, which the children of men builded.

The Lord could look across the entire world and see activities going on everywhere. Here he decides to get "up close and personal" with the people. It was not enough to just hear their voices or see their works. Rather it was necessary to truly understand what they were all about. What was behind their actions? What were their motives? The Lord saw that their hearts were set on personal gratification alone and he would be left out.

In Genesis chapter 18 we read the account of Abraham pleading with the Lord to spare Sodom, where his nephew Lot lived, from destruction. He asked for mercy for the city if 50 righteous people could be found; then 40,30, 20, and finally 10. The Lord agreed. Then is verse 20 we read these words:

20 And the Lord said, Because the cry of Sodom and Gomorrah is great, and because their sin is very grievous;

Again we see where the Lord came down to get first hand information before making a final decision. If he came down to see what was going on in our country today, what conclusions would he make? Would he be pleased? What if he came to see what was happening in your family, your workplace, or your church?

VERSE 6:
NOTHING WOULD BE IMPOSSIBLE

6 And the LORD said, Behold, the people is one, and they have all one language; and this they begin to do: and now nothing will be restrained from them, which they have imagined to do.

"The Lord said'" is an interesting phrase as it implies that he had an audience. He was not talking to the people at Babel. Rather it seems as he is conversing with others in heaven about what he saw during his visit. He saw everyone speaking with the same language endeavoring to build an empire, where all gratification would be for the people alone.

In addition, they had the power to actually accomplish the task they set out to do. When I first read this portion as a young Christian, I was absolutely floored. It said to me that collectively, we have the power to do anything. Prior to this account, the power of communication was not a barrier like we have today. Nevertheless, I remember thinking that if just the Christians around the world would join together, we could stop world hunger, stamp out disease, end conflicts between nations, and much more. Our creator gave us the ability to accomplish anything. Nothing would be impossible.

In Mark we read the story of the rich young ruler, who asked Jesus the question about how to get into heaven. After the man left, unwilling to give up his wealth, Jesus turned to his disciples and we read these words:

Mark 10 (NIV)

23 Jesus looked around and said to his disciples, "How hard it is for the rich to enter the kingdom of God!"

24 The disciples were amazed at his words. But Jesus said again, "Children, how hard it is to enter the kingdom of God!

25 It is easier for a camel to go through the eye of a needle than for a rich man to enter the kingdom of God."

26 The disciples were even more amazed, and said to each other, "Who then can be saved?"

27 Jesus looked at them and said, "With man this is impossible, but not with God; all things are possible with God."

Through Christ, all things are possible. That is something that I can count on, even when my own efforts fail.

VERSE 7:
GOD'S INTERVENTION

7 Go to, let us go down, and there confound their language, that they may not understand one another's speech.

Here we see the same action word "Go" followed by "let **us** go down", showing there was a unity in heaven on an action plan. Often in the ministry of Jesus on earth, our savior would go to the Father on our behalf. He was not here to do his will, but the father's. There was a continual sense of unity between Jesus, God's son, and God the father. I picture this scene as collaboration between them in heaven and an agreement was reached. Somehow, they must have looked at all that was happening at Babel and decided that the actions of the people would totally leave the creator out. Worship would be for others to do towards themselves, rather than what they would do towards God.

The committee in heaven decided to confuse their language so that they would no longer be able to have the kind of unity that they enjoyed. I found it interesting, that it does not say they could no longer accomplish what they set their hearts on. It is as though we still can achieve tremendous possibilities, but have to find new ways to communicate with one another. The dialects and languages of today are great, but there is one language that still exists and is universal, the language of love. If somehow the world can learn to speak in love again, I believe anything is still possible.

The decision was also not made in haste. Often we make judgments without getting all of the facts. This was not the case here. As human beings it is refreshing to know that our heavenly father does not act with the frustration or anger like we may act with our responses.

What is the language of your heart? Are you serving those around you or seeking to be served? This account lets us know that self-serving and self-centered communities are offensive to God, who desires to be an intricate part of our daily lives.

VERSE 8:
SCATTERED AGAIN

8 So the LORD scattered them abroad from thence upon the face of all the earth: and they left off to build the city.

Although there was an agreement in heaven, we see that it was the Lord who scattered the people and stopped the building process. In verse four we see that one of their purposes was to not be scattered. Here we see that is exactly what happened to them. Often we create our own punishment. I remember the story of Esther, Mordecai, and Haman, where the king asked Haman what punishment should be inflicted for a traitor. Haman thought the king was referring to Mordecai and therefore, made the punishment severe, only to find that it was meant for him (Esther 7:10). Someone once said that we need to be careful when we pray for more "patience" as we will get more trials to help teach us how to be patient. The people here were scattered as they lost the ability to communicate. Confusion was now the normal.

One of the interesting qualities societies need to have is "leadership". Somehow, mankind fails to focus on specific goals without someone or group to lead them. In some cases we fail to take a stand for something, without a place to retreat, if it doesn't work out. Responsibility is off our shoulders for something failing, when a higher authority commands it. I have seen worthwhile programs fail to be initiated in churches, because no one stepped up to chair them. Societies seem to need a soft place to fall or someone to blame when things don't go as planned. The people at Babel lost the leadership and were running around like the proverbial chicken without a head. Their only recourse was to go separate ways. The building process abruptly stopped.

VERSE 9:
MEMORIAL

9 Therefore is the name of it called Babel; because the LORD did there confound the language of all the earth: and from thence did the LORD scatter them abroad upon the face of all the earth.

Scripture repeats things that require emphasizing. This verse does just that. It is as though we need to take a special note of the lessons demonstrated at Babel. Confusion was created to counter a unity of purpose designed for personal gratification. We can take pride in many things like our family, achieving a college degree, serving our country, performance in the workplace, and much more. In each of these examples, we can also give thanks and praise to our creator for giving us the abilities needed to accomplish them. Babel demonstrated more than a prideful spirit. There was also a sense of pride that said "we can do anything without God, who created us".

Once again they found that they now were totally dependent on the Lord. Predators could be at their doors without anyone else to turn to for help. The Lord needed to break their spirit much like a parent does with a small child seeking to be in control. Brokenness is the beginning of a new healing.

The Lord's action went beyond Babel as the language of the whole world was affected. Does this mean that other areas of existence at the time outside of the Plain of Shinar would now be in confusion? Perhaps the Lord saw similar things rising with other areas of the world. Nevertheless, it was a hard lesson for the world to learn and we still need to understand it today.

HISTORICAL BACKGROUND

The Sons of Noah (Genesis 9)

*18 The sons of Noah who came out of the ark were **Shem**, **Ham** and **Japheth**. (Ham was the father of **Caanan**.)*

19 These were the three sons of Noah, and from them came the people who were scattered over the earth.

After the flood Noah and his family was directed to replenish the earth. Each son embarked in different directions as indicated by the words "scattered over the earth."

The account of Noah's drunkenness

Genesis 9:

20 And Noah began to be an husbandman, and he planted a vineyard:

21 And he drank of the wine, and was drunken; and he was uncovered within his tent.

*22 And Ham, the father of **Caanan**, saw the nakedness of his father, and told his two brethren without.*

23 And Shem and Japheth took a garment, and laid it upon both their shoulders, and went backward, and covered the nakedness of their father; and their faces were backward, and they saw not their father's nakedness.

24 And Noah awoke from his wine, and knew what his younger son had done unto him.

25 And he said, Cursed be **Caanan***; a servant of servants shall he be unto his brethren.*

26 And he said, Blessed be the LORD God of Shem; and **Caanan** *shall be his servant.*

27 God shall enlarge Japheth, and he shall dwell in the tents of Shem; and **Caanan** *shall be his servant.*

The story of Noah's drunkenness was one of those accounts that left me very troubled. Noah had passed out from too much to drink and was naked. I was taught in my upbringing that drinking too much intoxicating beverage was a sin. I found it difficult to picture the event. Here was a father, who was chosen by the creator to be spared from total world destruction in a flood, now without clothes and drunk. Noah went through a hundred years of mocking while building the ark. Through it all he remained faithful to God. As a new Christian this account made little sense to me. I can understand planting a vineyard and enjoying the fruits of his labor. Yet, somehow, this scene seemed to go beyond my understanding. Drunkenness was one thing, but the addition of nakedness left me with wonderment as a young Christian.

To top that off, we read about one son who saw his father's condition and made light of it, while the others acted in respect. I could understand that as a possibility with two brothers of my own. We don't always see things the same even now. Yet, my biggest problem came in Noah's reaction after he learned of Ham's response. Obviously he was upset and may have felt a high degree of disrespect. The thought of teaching Ham that it was wrong to dishonor him as a father would have been justified.

Then, the punishment was inflicted. Noah punished Ham by cursing his own son to a life of slavery. As a father I would try to make sure that the punishment fit the offence and was fair. This just didn't seem fair at all. If I could imagine being in Noah's condition, I could not contemplate taking his action, at least not for any length of time. At some point I would have to take some responsibility for being compromised like that in the first place. My son would have been the one whom I would have punished, but never my own grandchildren. It was an account that really left me with far more questions than answers.

Then there was the question; "Why would God put such an event in His word?" As I began to study, I learned that it was Ham's descendants that were there, seeking to call Babel their home. Genesis 9:18 points out ham's son, **Caanan**, specifically. Each of Noah's sons bore sons, but **Caanan** was singled out. It became clear that the questions that I had were tied together and that God had a lesson for even us today.

This account all took place while the sons were still close to their father. At some point afterwards they would begin their journeys apart. For Shem and Japheth there still may have been some method of communication going on as they may have been drawn closer by their father's praise for how they handled the situation. For Ham, the journey may well have left a bitter taste. I did not read of any account where Noah may have rescinded his curse. In fact, chapter nine ends with Noah's death.

Picture the situation where your own father rejects you, and told you will always serve your brothers. This is in stark contrast to a unified family working together to build an ark, based on a father's faith.

Have you ever felt rejected by your family?

GENERATIONS OF NOAH

Genesis 10: 1 – 31 (KJV)

1 Now these are the generations of the sons of Noah, Shem, Ham, and Japheth: and unto them were sons born after the flood.

Sons of Japheth

2 The sons of Japheth; Gomer, and Magog, and Madai, and Javan, and Tubal, and Meshech, and Tiras.

3 And the sons of Gomer; Ashkenaz, and Riphath, and Togarmah.

4 And the sons of Javan; Elishah, and Tarshish, Kittim, and Dodanim.

5 By these were the isles of the Gentiles divided in their lands; every one after his tongue, after their families, in their nations.

Sons of Ham

6 And the sons of Ham; Cush, and Mizraim, and Phut, and Caanan.

7 And the sons of Cush; Seba, and Havilah, and Sabtah, and Raamah, and Sabtecha: and the sons of Raamah; Sheba, and Dedan.

8 And Cush begat Nimrod: he began to be a mighty one in the earth.

9 He was a mighty hunter before the LORD: wherefore it is said, Even as Nimrod the mighty hunter before the LORD.

10 And the beginning of his kingdom was Babel, and Erech, and Accad, and Calneh, in the land of Shinar.

11 Out of that land went forth Asshur, and builded Nineveh, and the city Rehoboth, and Calah,

12 And Resen between Nineveh and Calah: the same is a great city.

13 And Mizraim begat Ludim, and Anamim, and Lehabim, and Naphtuhim,

14 And Pathrusim, and Casluhim, (out of whom came Philistim,) and Caphtorim.

15 And Caanan begat Sidon his firstborn, and Heth,

16 And the Jebusite, and the Amorite, and the Girgasite,

17 And the Hivite, and the Arkite, and the Sinite,

18 And the Arvadite, and the Zemarite, and the Hamathite: and afterward were the families of the Caananites spread abroad.

19 And the border of the Caananites was from Sidon, as thou comest to Gerar, unto Gaza; as thou goest, unto Sodom, and Gomorrah, and Admah, and Zeboim, even unto Lasha.

20 These are the sons of Ham, after their families, after their tongues, in their countries, and in their nations.

Sons of Shem

21 Unto Shem also, the father of all the children of Eber, the brother of Japheth the elder, even to him were children born.

22 The children of Shem; Elam, and Asshur, and Arphaxad, and Lud, and Aram.

23 And the children of Aram; Uz, and Hul, and Gether, and Mash.

24 And Arphaxad begat Salah; and Salah begat Eber.

25 And unto Eber were born two sons: the name of one was Peleg; for in his days was the earth divided; and his brother's name was Joktan.

26 And Joktan begat Almodad, and Sheleph, and Hazarmaveth, and Jerah,

27 And Hadoram, and Uzal, and Diklah,

28 And Obal, and Abimael, and Sheba,

29 And Ophir, and Havilah, and Jobab: all these were the sons of Joktan.

30 And their dwelling was from Mesha, as thou goest unto Sephar a mount of the east.

31 These are the sons of Shem, after their families, after their tongues, in their lands, after their nations.

To curse anyone has always been wrong for me. We may say things in a vehicle while driving that would be considered cursing towards drivers who act disrespectful towards us, but we only hurt ourselves. They probably didn't hear what we said. The only way they would even know we were displeased with them is through a gesture or loud horn. I have long since learned that we are far better off letting it go, thanking God that no one was hurt, and moving on. Yet, that is not what Noah did. The curse was final. Ham's descendants would be servants, and a servant's life during those times was without honor. Shem and

Japheth would have extended territory for their families, while Ham would have only a life of servanthood to look forward to. What a blow. Verse one indicates that these children were born after the flood. Noah may have been enjoying the fruits of his labors with the vineyard, but also with a wealth of grandchildren.

I found it very interesting that Ham has more verses covering his family tree (vs 6 – 21) than either Japheth (1 – 5) or Shem (22 – 32). Usually, this is not a coincidence. When God wants us to understand something significant, emphasis is made accordingly. Later, we will investigate some deeper aspects of this, but for now we have the events that led to the account of the Tower at Babel.

Note some of the cities that Ham's descendants were associated with:

Babylon, Sodom, Gomorrah, Nineveh... was the curse real?

A FATHER'S LEADERSHIP

As a father, one of the areas that I find as a daily challenge is in my leadership for my children. There have been times when situations that justified some form of punishment for wrongdoing, was approached with a wrong response. I may have acted hastily without knowing all of the facts or in anger, where I responded blindly. I have learned over the years that either reaction could create undesired consequences. Instead of my children learning respect for my leadership and a lesson for their actions, they would have learned to be afraid of me. That was something that I did not desire and needed to rectify.

First, I needed to maintain a level playing field. I could not jump to quick conclusions or allow my own feelings (frustration, fear) lead to anger. I needed to find ways to calmly approach situations and allow some amount of time to pass to gather my thoughts and feelings in a loving way. After all, these are my flesh and blood. I would not want to cause myself harm. Even more, I would not want my children to be fearful of me at any time.

Second, I always desire to improve as a father. If I have created fear instead of love or respect, then I need to take the necessary steps to rectify things. When I act impulsively, I am out of control. My children need to look up to their father and the fear they may see can cause them to want to look away. They need to know they are loved. They need to hear their father's remorse for inappropriate behavior towards them. I need to lovingly seek forgiveness from them, embrace them, and learn self-control in the future.

This has been an on-going process for me as I am sure it is for many dads out there. The rewards are great in the development of loving, self-assured, and devout children. Children are truly gifts from God. God looked down on Jesus during his baptism in the Jordan and said:

Matt.3:16 – 17 (KJV)

> 16 *And Jesus, when he was baptized, went up straightway out of the water: and, lo, the heavens were opened unto him, and he saw the Spirit of God descending like a dove, and lighting upon him:*

> 17 *And lo a voice from heaven, saying, This is my beloved Son, in whom I am well pleased.*

What a joy it is when we can echo those words for our children.

NOAH'S LEADERSHIP

During the time leading up to the flood, Noah demonstrated resolve in building an ark without any water in sight. He showed that he was faithful to the God that he believed would watch over him and his family. When the flood came his family recognized that his faith was real. The flood came and they stayed in the ark with their father. The closeness, perhaps, led to an even deeper understanding for Noah. Noah earned their respect and love.

So why did the inspired word of God include the scene with Noah naked and drunk in the middle of the family account of his sons. This seemed strange to me until I read the 'Prayer of Jabez" by Bruce Wilkerson. A few obscure verses seemed to appear in a long list of begats.

1 Chronicles 4: 9 – 10 (KJV)

9 And Jabez was more honorable than his brethren: and his mother called his name Jabez, saying, Because I bare him with sorrow.."

10 And Jabez called on the God of Israel, saying, Oh that thou wouldest bless me indeed, and enlarge my coast, and that thine hand might be with me, and that thou wouldest keep me from evil, that it may not grieve me! And God granted him that which he requested.

Bruce showed that it was no accident that they were there. I believe that it was also more than coincidence that Noah's account was recorded for us to learn from. This was the story of a father who may have been like any of us. He felt betrayed by his son, Ham. He felt disrespected. He responded, perhaps without fully understanding all of the facts. Although I still struggle with how a father can curse his son and even worse curse his grandson, the actions are still recorded.

Ham went on to lead generations with negative results. Sodom and Gomorrah was so wicked that not even 10 righteous people could be found there to spare it from God's wrath.

Gen.18: 32 (KJV)

32 And he said, Oh let not the Lord be angry, and I will speak yet but this once: Peradventure ten shall be found there. And he said, I will not destroy it for ten's sake.

The cities were so far removed from a faith in God that the devil himself must have been overjoyed.

Gen. 19: 23 – 25 (KJV)

23 The sun was risen upon the earth when Lot entered into Zoar.

24 Then the LORD rained upon Sodom and upon Gomorrah brimstone and fire from the LORD out of heaven;

25 And he overthrew those cities, and all the plain, and all the inhabitants of the cities, and that which grew upon the ground.

Nineveh was also in need of reform as the Lord sent Jonah to warn them to repent. Even Jonah first refused as if to say, "Why bother". The wickedness there was renown.

Jonah 1:1-3 (NIV)

1 Now the word of the LORD came unto Jonah the son of Amittai, saying,

2 Arise, go to Nineveh, that great city, and cry against it; for their wickedness is come up before me.

3 But Jonah rose up to flee unto Tarshish from the presence of the LORD, and went down to Joppa; and he found a ship going to Tarshish: so he paid the fare thereof, and went down into it, to go with them unto Tarshish from the presence of the LORD.

Somehow, without a father's love, a son learns to rely on others or himself to go on. Past teachings are lost. Godly principles are replaced with human ones which fall well short. Generations of people that follow stray even further.

I believe that this account was placed in Genesis to be an example for what could happen when we move away from the father's leadership. I believe that from the very beginning we had a creator, who desired more than anything to be our source of every good and nourishing thing for our enjoyment. I believe that we are not perfect, like Noah and need to be in an attitude of repentance at all times. When we cause someone else to fall away from God, we need to seek the Lord's help to make things right again. We have such an awesome responsibility to rear our children in a Godly way and can only do so with divine help. This account reminds us that we are imperfect and can only be made perfect through the blood of Christ. It also teaches us that when left to our own choices we will fail. God's Word is filled with people who served Him faithfully and still fell short of perfection, like David, Moses, or Sampson to name a few. Noah was no different.

What messages are you sending to your children?

Our words or actions may lead others towards Christ or away. We may not be able to control the fertility of the soil, but we still need to plant the seeds. God will take care of the nurturing. Sodom and Gomorrah may have had "Rocky" soil, but the warnings were still there to repent. Nineveh also received similar warnings from Jonah and the people chose to repent. We need to plant good seeds, especially for our children, if there is to be an abundant harvest in the future.

ENOUGH ALREADY

Actress Jennifer Lopez played the role of a wife, who was abused and controlled by her husband in the movie "Enough". She finally stood up and took a stand against him. Often that is not the case and deep emotional scars are created. These scars can cause extremely negative consequences like suicide. They can cripple our spirit from ever achieving our goals and may even prevent us from having goals.

Psychologists have documented how women who have been abused as children accept their role in life as sub-servant. They stay in abusive marriages for the duration, because they believe they are not worthy of men. Any man that would have them is better than no man at all, even with the belittlement and abuse. Until they understand that their belief is not true and take new steps to change, they will stay in their misery.

The people at Babel had reached that point and were saying "Enough is enough". They were taking their stand at the Plain of Shinar. They had enough:

- Wandering
- Disrespect
- Lack of appreciation
- Feeling sub-standard, unloved

This new city would not only be their stand against past set backs, but it would be a statement of their desire for change. The stand was saying:

- We are to be respected
- We are not servants to others
- We can do anything that we put our hearts and minds into
- We are to be recognized for great achievements
- We are to be envied
- We are important

Pearl Harbor Lesson

The Japanese attacked American vessels at Pearl Harbor with a fierce intensity. They had a mission that they literally would die for and use aircraft as bombs. America was caught off guard. The battle front was on the other side of the globe, but America took a new stand in the Pacific. The retaliation was swift and even more deadly. The Japanese resolve and spirit was crushed. History has many examples of people who overcome adversities, persevere, and reach new heights. The small island of Japan is now a recognized world economic leader. Honda and Toyota are synonymous with high quality and durability standards in the automobile industry. American manufacturers have had to "retool" to stay competitive.

We said "enough is enough" when they attacked our fleet. They said it when they gathered themselves and created a new purpose.

People like Chuck Norris, who started an inner city karate program, or Jay Mcgraw (Dr. Phil's son), who is working to stamp out bullying in America's schools are rising up saying "enough is enough". Being a veteran of the Viet Nam War era, I was encouraged to see our vets given the respect they deserved. Our military is fighting a war on terror after September 11, 2001 and are getting their heroes welcome from a proud country. This list could be exhausting for people who have risen above their demons and cried "enough already".

Noah cursed Ham and his descendents and here they are shouting the same chant. One of the reasons that I believe this account was placed between the lineages of Noah's sons is that God desired for us to see how our words/actions can have long term affects. These can be positive or they can be catastrophic. Rebellion is often the result of being hurt until the pain or sorrow is too much to bear. Self worth, or lack of it, can send us out of control or cause us to reach new heights of achievement.

Armed with God's promises, Noah and his son's were sent out into a new world to repopulate it. The solitude of being in the ark for about a year may have established a new appreciation for life and the creator. Noah issued a curse towards Ham and blessings towards Shem and Japheth. Then we begin to see the consequences. We can speculate on what the world would have been like if Noah came to his senses and restored a loving relationship with Ham, but the Bible does not indicate that it ever happened.

What about today? Are we any different than Noah? Are we building up our children as loving parents or creating unresolved issues with them? I believe that the number one thing children desire from their parents is to feel loved and accepted for who they are. We cannot try to make them into people we would have liked them to be, as if they relive our childhood as we would have liked it. We cannot provide all the worldly goods for them without spending time with them. Mom's who make the choice to stay home instead of making an extra income can be heroes to their children, which has no price tag. It is a sad thing to watch people alienate themselves from their parents. Yet, it is all too commonplace.

Sadness overtakes the families of suicide victims, when loved ones say "enough is enough", especially when there is no warning. Without hope, dying is seen as relief. The people at Babel saw new hope in the land at Shinar. They turned despair into unified strength. Like the story of the "Little Train That Could", they shouted "yes we can". From the account we don't read where God condemned their desires, only their purpose. Saul's zealousness to stop the spread of Christianity was used to benefit the spread of it, when his purpose was confronted (Acts 9). Saul became known as Paul. God could have said "enough already" to Paul and simply stopped the persecution. How much better would the world be today if the purposes of man aligned with those of our creator?

CREATOR'S VIEW

It might be fun to try and picture the scene in heaven and the discussion that took place over the events at Shinar. The Creator may have been surrounded by heavenly beings or simply having a father-son talk. I can imagine this talk going something like this:

Father: What do you see down there son?

Son: There sure are a lot of people scurrying around since the flood subsided.

Father: Noah and his sons have been faithful repopulating the earth again.

Son: They seem to be separating in new directions forming new towns along the way.

Father: That's right, but along the way they have maintained some common areas. They all speak the same language. That wasn't the case before the flood and look what happened.

Son: Communication is a good thing, huh?

Father: I sure enjoy our little talks.

Son: Yeah!

Father: Look down there on the Plain of Shinar and tell me what you see.

Son: It looks like everyone is working together to build a high monument. What do you think that means?

Father: People used to build false Gods (idols) to worship instead of their Creator. This is different as these people are on some kind of ego trip.

Son: That doesn't sound like a good thing.

Father: No, it isn't. They are making a statement like "We are important, self-sufficient, and don't need anyone else".

Son: They sure are very prideful.

Father: Pride can be a good thing. I am sure proud of you, son. There will come a time when I will tell the whole world that you are my son "In whom I am well pleased". I am a proud father. Pride can also lead down a path to destruction and I am afraid that is where these people are headed.

Son: What do you mean, father?

Father: Well, today they are building a city with a watch tower. In itself that is a good thing. But when people come to see all that they have accomplished with their hard work, they will let them know how good it is. Each time pride is nourished and the response is "We can do anything". Where does that leave you and me son?

Son: We will be forgotten for sure. Communication between us would cease and that would separate us. We sure desire to be a part of their lives. Don't they know how much richer their lives could be if we did that?

Father: Not anymore son. The generations to follow will not be taught about us, only about what was done by their ancestors. The account of the flood would be forgotten and lost.

Son: We went through this before. You spared Noah and his family only to see this?

Father: It was our hope that these new generations would have grown closer to us. We never changed or moved, but they moved from us. Pride will do that if left unchecked.

Son: Could we have done something different?

Father: It's all about choices, son. We knew that was a risky gift for them to have a free will, but it was the only way they could truly love us in return like we love them. What if they applied the same intensity building the tower, instead to eliminate hunger in the world?

Son: There sure is enough food to go around.

Father: That's right, son, but again we see pride hoarding these things.

Son: This is just one city. What can we do?

Father: We could send a lightning bolt and destroy the tower.

Son: Yes, but they would probably band together again and rebuild it. After all they wouldn't think the lightning was an act of their creator.

Father: We could cause great confusion that would break their unity. If they no longer could communicate with each other, the bricks would not be strong; the mortar would be applied at the wrong time, and everything else. Then the building process would stop altogether.

Son: That would create havoc.

Father: More than that, it would once again separate them. They would have to go off in small groups with some ability to communicate and seek new places to live. Only those who spoke the same dialect would conjugate.

Son: That would crush their pride, huh?

Father: For a time, son; for a time.

Father-Son talks:

Father – Son chats over the years are seen as deep rewarding experiences. Not only does it help each person know where the other stands on a given subject, but also addresses their level of passion. Somehow, I picture the creator of the universe sharing in a manner that anyone observing would see a glow on both of their faces. Those times are special for most of us. Noah lost that with his son Ham, when he passed on the curse after he felt disgraced (Gen.10:27-29).

We have a father in heaven that loves us more than any earthly father can. He created us in his image (love). He singled man (male and female) out for a special place in all of creation. He gave us an eternal soul and all of the things we need to communicate with him. He lets us know that he cares for us so much that he desires to adopt each of us as his own child with all of the privileges that go with it. His arms were open wide when he sent his only true son to the cross to die for us. Yet, he is a righteous father, who wants only the best for us. He knows that when we fall short, we need to be corrected. He is always there for us to go to and desires and welcomes each opportunity for us to seek him.

Made in God's Image: Genesis 1:25-27 (KJV)

25 And God made the beast of the earth after his kind, and cattle after their kind, and every thing that creepeth upon the earth after his kind: and God saw that it was good.

26 And God said, Let us make man in our image, after our likeness: and let them have dominion over the fish of the sea, and over the fowl of the air, and over the cattle, and over all the earth, and over every creeping thing that creepeth upon the earth.

27 *So God created man in his own image, in the image of God created he him; male and female created he them.*

These people went away from his presence. Everything he tried to do to get them to call on him was lost in their own selfish desires. This scene in heaven, though imagined, serves to illustrate that everything was examined thoroughly before the action to cast confusion on the people was initiated. These people had probably been building the city and tower for a long time. It was not an instantaneous decision to stop it before it started. As a father, I would want to give my children every opportunity to change a wrong doing before inflicting harsh punishment. Genesis 11:5 says, ***"But the LORD came down to see the city and the tower that the men were building."*** He analyzed their physical achievements as well as their motives.

God does not act impulsively, but with love and patience. He desires for each of us to see him as a safe haven. In this account the road back to him was cut off. The people were so far away from him that something had to be done or they would forever have been lost from his presence. The decision was made to confuse them, rather than destroy them. Even here he demonstrated that he still loved them.

DENNIS A. MCINTYRE

ACTING HASTILY

The evidence was examined, options were on the table, and a decision was reached. How often do we as parents make hasty decisions?

I remember the time when a co-worker shared a story with me about his wife and daughter. He said that he arrived home one evening and found his wife all upset. She explained that she found an empty cigarette case in their daughter's dresser when she put away some clean clothes. The daughter was about 16 years old and was instructed that she was never to smoke. The mother had stewed about it most of the day and unleashed a verbal assault of her husband, who was instructed to do something about it. Smoking was not to be tolerated in that home.

Dad heard the evidence, went to her room, and confronted the daughter. The conversation went something like this:

For simplicity we will give them both names.

Ron: Rhonda, you know how much your mother and I will not tolerate smoking. It is an addictive habit, unhealthy, discolors your teeth, and much more.

Rhonda: Of course I do, papa.

Ron: Today, while putting away your clothes, your mother found an empty cigarette wrapper in your drawer. She is really upset about it and so am I.

Rhonda: Did you see the wrapper dad?

Ron: No, but your mom wouldn't lie about that.

Rhonda: (after going over and retrieving the wrapper) Here it is. Take a look at it. My friend gave me her phone number today and it was the only thing I could find to write on.

Ron: (after viewing the wrapper) I'm sorry. I guess I should have examined everything before coming to my confusion. I guess mom and I need to trust you more, huh? Will you forgive us?

Rhonda: Of course I forgive you guys.

God has all the facts and makes decisions with our best interests at heart. It would not be a good thing for his creation to continue serving themselves alone. Great things can be accomplished when people work together, but there must be the right motives. Leaving God out will produce ultimate failure.

1. Why is it that when people reach their lowest point in life, they seem to cry out instinctively, "Oh God?"

_____

_____

_____

_____

2. What would the conversation in heaven be like if the focus was on your family.

_____

_____

_____

3. What would you want to be said?

_____

_____

_____

_____

4. Are these opposing of coinciding?

_____

_____

_____

_____

Barrier of Language

The communication process can be a joy or a nightmare. When our daughter became a mother she used her skills as a special education teacher to help make the interaction with her children a pleasant one. The sound of a screaming child is not only hard on the ears, but also not understandable. She began teaching sign language to her son. I remember how well he seemed to get his desires across. Rarely did I hear any discontent and even then it was usually something that had not yet had a way to be expressed. By the time he was able to talk, he was already beyond his age in communication development. He would even make new signs for mom and dad to understand.

When our desires and thoughts are effectively communicated, we tend to feel good. Anxiety and frustration cause us to feel less satisfied. We tend to elevate our voices or find other ways to get our message across, usually causing even more anxiety. Eventually we get angry and communication is impossible.

The Red Truck

I remember many years ago hearing about a Stanford graduate who wrote his thesis on communication breakdowns in people. His premise was that the human machine takes in 10, 20, or 100 times more information than it gives out in speech. Information comes in all forms like sound, touch, body language, inflections, etc. He further theorized that in some people this process gets short circuited and without knowing it, people try to speak much faster than they would normally.

In other words, the processing that takes place after information is received is bypassed.

To test his theory he went to a children's day care center and observed a little boy (about 3 or 4) screaming uncontrollably in a room by himself. The staff was beside itself as they tried everything they could to calm him down and understand what he was trying to communicate. The man brought a state of the art taping system and taped the boy's voice. Then he used the system to play it back at a much slower rate. The high pitched screams began to be discernible and he heard the words "Red Truck". He looked into the room and noticed high on one of the shelves a small toy red truck. After retrieving it he gave it to the boy and the reaction was instantaneous. The boy stopped yelling and looked content as he played with his new toy.

This story touched me deeply at the time. It taught me a great deal about our need to be understood. I wonder even now, whether this student's work has spurned new research for psychologists to use to help others. The illustration does serve to offer an important lesson on human development. When we are understood and accepted, we feel better, even empowered. When the communication process is solid, great things are possible.

> 6 And the LORD said, Behold, the people is one, and they have all one language; and this they begin to do: and now nothing will be restrained from them, which they have imagined to do.

German anyone?

Another illustration came at the end of our daughter's junior year in High School. Through the year we entertained an exchange student from Germany, who wanted to improve her skills in English. She did very well in that area and we were able to communicate with ease. In the last month of her stay her mother also joined us in our home. She spoke little or no English and I was limited with my German. Most of the time, her daughter translated for both of us.

One night I was left with her mom for the evening with only a German-English / English-German dictionary to help us converse. By the end of the night we were laughing and calm. Somehow we were able to get our thoughts across by pointing to words in the other's language using the dictionary. There were times of frustration, but we were up to the challenge. If we had to work together and build a city, it would certainly have been a disaster. We also tried to draw pictures, make gestures, and other creative areas to get our point across. Both of us desired to communicate and made the effort to understand the other. The time was a wonderful test of the human spirit.

Barriers can be opportunities. They exist in all relationships. How people deal with them can make the challenge enjoyable or chaotic. A husband may ask his wife how her day went and get an unexpected response or a normal one. A simple "It was Ok" may mean "You don't want to know" or "Everything went wrong, but I don't want to burden you with my problems". A wife may want the conversation to continue with more questions, but the husband may only be asking to distill any tension from his day. Often the process creates a barrier as each other's feelers are not sensed. These barriers are not because of the language, as both partners are perfectly able to understand the other's words. Rather their words are chosen to not cause anxiety, and allow for a continuation.

"It was Ok" may be a cue for the husband to ask another question like "Tell me more." The wife may add a short tidbit about one portion of her day and wait for a new response or question. The more she feels there is safe ground, the longer the communication lasts. When everyone has shared what they needed to share, the barrier breaks down. Often this is not the case and one or both partners feel dissatisfied. The next episode starts with a small wall. Each time, when the conversation stops prematurely, another brick is added to the wall. Eventually, a verbal explosion, totally unrelated to the conversation takes place and one partner is bewildered.

Are there any barriers in your relationship with your spouse; your children; your co-workers? We would say yes to that question if we prematurely ended a conversation. But how would we know about the other person(s)? When the words "I'm Ok" are the last words spoken by each party, then things are probably not ok.

Jesus spoke on a hill in Galilee. 5000 people heard, understood, and committed themselves to follow Christ. These people were there ready, willing, and able to hear what he had to say. They knew of his miracles. They were spiritually hungry. They put aside their own agenda to just listen to Jesus. They were not there to debate. No barriers existed and the words spoken penetrated their hearts.

At other times Jesus would speak in parables (stories with a lesson). He knew whose heart was open to listen. Those who heard, properly interpreted, and applied his teachings left joyful. Those people, like the Pharisees, had personal agendas and missed the point. Jesus knew who would understand because he knew their heart. He knew who truly desired to understand the teachings of God and those who wanted to defend their own desires. Those who understood received more. Those who did not went away empty and lost.

A Lesson about Barriers

Psychologists have concluded that only 8-10% of what is said gets processed by those who listen. That number goes up considerably when other senses are added like sight, sound, touch, body languages, etc. One of my favorite ice breakers (with a group) illustrates this concept. I would ask for a volunteer from the group to describe something to the others using only words. That person would speak from a place in the room that was out of their sight, and would use words that would help them draw the object. Words like "glass" or "plastic" could not be used. Words like "left, up, line, curve" were OK. Everyone else would attempt to draw the object and then guess what it was. Occasionally, I would offer a prize to the first person who guessed correctly. Rarely would I have to deliver the prize.

Therefore, we cannot assume that what we are saying is being interpreted as we intended. The phrase "Pictures say a thousand words" applies as the more ways we can illustrate our points, the better chances we have to be properly understood. Teachers require good feedback from their students to know that they are being the most effective. Spouses can share what they thought they heard with the other.

Parents can stop demanding perfection and listen more to their children. One-way communications can be called lectures. Interpretations become left to each individual. Since we come from a wide variety of backgrounds, rarely will our interpretation be consistent.

When the Lord came down to see what was happening at the tower site, the people were in unity. Somehow, they had heard the principles of good communication and applied them. Barriers to this process were minimal or non-existent. It must have been like the old married couple, which knew what each other wanted, with hardly a word uttered. They had learned over the years what the signals were and responded accordingly. Breaking down the language created an instant barrier and the people became confused. Once again they were scattered.

Today, we have countries all over the world, which speak different dialects, even with a common language. We see immigrants trying to keep their languages and not desire to learn that of the country they are entering. We see cities with ethnic sectors, because the people band together to maintain their cultures and languages. Television and radio stations create ways to reach these diverse groups, to raise advertising dollars. Add to this mix the political agendas that want their votes and we have created a barrier maze of sorts.

It amazes this writer that unity comes with catastrophe. A natural disaster brings people together regardless of their cultural or ethnic backgrounds. In 1991 in upstate New York, our family experienced an ice storm. People lost their power for days / weeks. When the cold snap passed, homes would flood without electricity to run the sump pumps. People came out of the woodwork to assist their neighbors, despite any language barrier. Love and compassion was universal. Once the power was restored and it was business as usual, people returned to their sanctuaries and isolated states.

Our creator seeks to communicate with his creation. He gave us his word. His son, Jesus came down to live as a human and shared the desires of the father. We can choose to keep the doors open and let God in or we can keep them closed. He hates barriers that keep him away. The people at Babel had closed the doors. God didn't move from them. They turned from him.

He is always near:

Rev. 3:19 – 21(KJV)

19 As many as I love, I rebuke and chasten: be zealous therefore, and repent.

20 Behold, I stand at the door, and knock: if any man hear my voice, and open the door, I will come in to him, and will sup with him, and he with me.

21 To him that overcometh will I grant to sit with me in my throne, even as I also overcame, and am set down with my Father in his throne.

Matt.28: 16 – 20

16 Then the eleven disciples went away into Galilee, into a mountain where Jesus had appointed them.

17 And when they saw him, they worshipped him: but some doubted.

18 And Jesus came and spake unto them, saying, All power is given unto me in heaven and in earth.

19 Go ye therefore, and teach all nations, baptizing them in the name of the Father, and of the Son, and of the Holy Ghost:

20 Teaching them to observe all things whatsoever I have commanded you: and, lo, I am with you alway, even unto the end of the world. Amen.

DENNIS A. MCINTYRE

SCATTERED AGAIN

Building the city meant no more wandering to Ham's descendents. They would have a place to call home. It would be a place of safety, security, acceptance, and love. Having a home meant building roots in the earth to keep them from being blown away in the wind. That was their desire and purpose. Now the dream was shattered again.

Over the years our family looked forward to getting away on vacations. The anticipation was filled with excitement, yet we always knew we would come back home when it was over. At some point the excitement waned and we again looked forward to returning home. Home was that place where somehow we felt safe, secure, loved, accepted, and much more. Perhaps we shared the joys of the vacation trips more because of the bonds we had at home. Yet, each time we returned, we had a new higher appreciation for the place we left.

The people at Babel never had that experience. Home was a desert stop over. Vacations were something in a dream. Safety and security were daily reminders of what they longed for. They were continuously on the move, seeking acceptance. As descendents of Ham the chastisement of Noah still was their curse.

Gen.9:24 – 27 (KJV)

24 And Noah awoke from his wine, and knew what his younger son had done unto him.

*25 And he said, **Cursed be Caanan**; a **servant of servants** shall he be unto his brethren.*

*26 And he said, Blessed be the LORD God of Shem; and **Caanan shall be his servant.***

*27 God shall enlarge Japheth, and he shall dwell in the tents of Shem; and **Caanan shall be his servant.***

They felt:

- Abandoned
- Unworthiness
- Insecurity
- Anger / frustration

Their lives were certainly far from being filled with joy, until they came to the Plain of Shinar. At that point ecstasy, hope, and pride leaped in their hearts. The idea of separation was the furthest thing on their minds.

Now everything was upside down. People were speaking, but only a few could understand. Those small groups, who had some recognition of the language spoken, gathered whatever they had and left on a new journey. Everyone disbanded leaving the hopes and dreams behind. The city of hope became a vivid reminder of shattered hope. The tower was now a tombstone marking the burial site.

WHAT DID THIS ACCOMPLISH?

The question remains; did they return back to the Lord for the hope they lost? The confusion in language caused them to refocus on the basics. God was still with them, whether they looked to him for help or not. Nature still revealed a creator. Faith in their own abilities was lost and they needed to believe in something else to survive every day challenges.

This story impressed me in another way. God could have destroyed the city. He did so with Sodom and Gomorrah. Jericho's walls came down without a fight. He is all-powerful and certainly capable of such an act, but he didn't. He simply confused them. He broke their spirit of pride. Their unity was lost. If God was so upset with all that was going on, then why didn't he destroy them? The answer is the same then as it is today. God is absolutely in love with his creation. He created mankind in his own image. He breathed his own breath into Adam (an account only recorded for man). He simply desired for creation to love him back.

Sodom and Gomorrah's Wickedness: Gen.18:20 (KJV)

20 And the LORD said, Because the cry of Sodom and Gomorrah is great, and because their sin is very grievous;

Sodom and Gomorrah's Destruction: Gen.19:23-25 (KJV)

23 The sun was risen upon the earth when Lot entered into Zoar.

24 Then the LORD rained upon Sodom and upon Gomorrah brimstone and fire from the LORD out of heaven;

25 And he overthrew those cities, and all the plain, and all the inhabitants of the cities, and that which grew upon the ground.

Fall of Jericho: Heb.11:30 (KJV)

30 By faith the walls of Jericho fell down, after they were compassed about seven days.

Breath of God into man: Gen.2:7 (KJV)

7 And the LORD God formed man of the dust of the ground, and breathed into his nostrils the breath of life; and man became a living soul.

Jesus came to live as one of us. He understands our hearts, our thoughts, and everything else about us. His message spoke about things like hope, joy, peace, and love. He constantly told us to not be afraid, as he is here to bring peace and comfort. He knows us better than we know ourselves. He tells us that he came to "seek and save the lost" (Luke 19:10) and gives abundant life. These are not the words of someone bent on our destruction. These are words that the people at Babel needed to hear all along, but something kept them from listening. These are the same words that are desirous today, but the world is also not listening. God is patiently waiting for even one to return to him and when that happens, there is great rejoicing in heaven.

Unity can be a great thing to behold. God's word speaks of two people being one in the marriage ceremony. Where two or more people gather in the name of the lord and pray, great things can be accomplished. God the father, son and spirit live in perfect unity. The unity on display at Babel was different as God was left out. The God of Noah betrayed them and they wandered away. God did not desire to destroy them. He only wanted for them to rethink who they are, where they are headed, and who can lead them. He wanted to be their source of strength. He desired to guide them. Now they were scattered, but able to call on his name once again. Perhaps some did.

QUEST FOR UNITY

Unity is a concept that has been around since creation. Human beings have an inane desire to live in a world without chaos, where peace and tranquility are desired over war and confusion. When the people came to the Plain of Shinar, they longed for something that would unite them emotionally, psychologically, physically, and socially. Up to that point they were confused, lost, and considered outcasts. Safety and security would have been something to dream about as, perhaps, they were ever concerned about what lay ahead. Banding together at Shinar was more than just taking a stand. The city was to be fortified with a wall and a tower that was more than a place to watch for unwanted visitors. The stand was unified by their desires for recognition as a people with something to offer the world and not as outcasts.

The world is also full of people who work alone. These people do not want help from others. They are filled with self-confidence and pride that makes them set goals or strive for a positive end result. These people may accomplish great worldly tasks and never understand the concept of "Unity". For societies to truly flourish, people need to unite.

A House Divided

"A house divided against itself cannot stand." (Abraham Lincoln)

The words of Abraham Lincoln at his Gettysburg Address, were focused on a separated country. The war between the north and south had driven a stake into the heart of America. The country's Declaration of Independence assured life, liberty, and the pursuit of happiness to all. The issue of slavery was in violation of those rights. President Lincoln's message clearly stated that such a division in a society would not create strength, but rather ultimate defeat. America needed to put her differences aside and work together if it was to remain strong.

Matt. 12:22-30 (KJV)

22 Then was brought unto him one possessed with a devil, blind, and dumb: and he healed him, insomuch that the blind and dumb both spake and saw.

24 But when the Pharisees heard this, they said, "It is only by Beelzebub, the prince of demons, that this fellow drives out demons."

23 And all the people were amazed, and said, Is not this the son of David?

24 But when the Pharisees heard it, they said, This fellow doth not cast out devils, but by Beelzebub the prince of the devils.

*25 And Jesus knew their thoughts, and said unto them, **Every kingdom divided against itself is brought to desolation; and every city or house divided against itself shall not stand:***

26 And if Satan cast out Satan, he is divided against himself; how shall then his kingdom stand?

27 And if I by Beelzebub cast out devils, by whom do your children cast them out? therefore they shall be your judges.

28 But if I cast out devils by the Spirit of God, then the kingdom of God is come unto you.

29 Or else how can one enter into a strong man's house, and spoil his goods, except he first bind the strong man? and then he will spoil his house.

30 He that is not with me is against me; and he that gathereth not with me scattereth abroad.

Jesus was making two points here. First, he was speaking to the religious leaders of his time, who did not accept him as being from god. They called him a follower of Satan (Beelzebub), and his power to drive out demons came from the devil. Jesus questioned them, by saying that it would be pointless to drive out your own demons. Such a work would defeat your own purpose.

Second, he was referring to driving out demons by the "Spirit of God", which would allow God's kingdom to be established where the demon dwelt. He further illustrated the concept to them by comparing the situation to a strong man, who would need to be bound before anyone could take his possessions.

The principle is universal. Far more can be accomplished in this world when people unite for a common cause, then when they are in disarray. We only need to look at the family unit to see where barriers begin. Then look at schools, churches, government bodies, and the list goes on. A unified America to Mr. Lincoln would result in a strong America once again. People would have to put aside their differences and seek a higher place.

The basic building block for unity in a society is the family unit. If people cannot find peace and tranquility in their own homes, how can we expect it in a nation filled with broken homes? The divorce rate alone in America is staggering.

Synergy:

The word "synergy" applies to the kind of unity that helps describe a godly unity. In simple terms it means together two can do more than twice as much as either one. We could say one plus one is three. The bigger picture speaks of far more than that. We can view how this works in nature.

Two oxen:

A single ox may be able to pull 800 pounds with ropes and a harness. Farmers used them to plow fields or pull carts. Loads greater than that, would require yoking two or more animals together. An amazing discovery happened. When two were yoked together, they were able to pull over 2000 pounds. Something happened that not only allowed them to pull more than 2.5 times the load, but they did it with more ease. In other words, the animals drew upon each other for more strength and stamina.

Geese:

Most of us have seen the formations of geese as they fly south to escape winter cold. They form a "V" with a single goose leading and the others following close behind. On the surface it looks like a family trip, but far more is happening than that. A single goose may be able to fly 100 miles in a day without getting exhausted. Each new day may cause the miles to reduce by fatigue. The formation has an interesting phenomenon. One by one the geese change positions. The lead goose falls back to the end of the line while a new one moves up to take the position. The cycle continues for the entire trip. The energy spent by each goose is a fraction of what it would have been if they all flew alone. Geese that are not in the lead draft on the one in front, much like a race car in a race. This allows them to travel just as fast as those in front, without expending as much energy. This process allows them to all fly together much further than they could have separately. (One account that I read indicated 50 – 70% farther)

Our creator has placed many examples in nature to help us understand how important it is to work together. We can accomplish far more when we apply our individual gifts and talents. Jesus tells us that we are all different parts of one body.

1 Cor.12:12 – 31 (KJV)

12 For as the body is one, and hath many members, and all the members of that one body, being many, are one body: so also is Christ.

13 For by one Spirit are we all baptized into one body, whether we be Jews or Gentiles, whether we be bond or free; and have been all made to drink into one Spirit.

14 For the body is not one member, but many.

15 If the foot shall say, Because I am not the hand, I am not of the body; is it therefore not of the body?

16 And if the ear shall say, Because I am not the eye, I am not of the body; is it therefore not of the body?

17 If the whole body were an eye, where were the hearing? If the whole were hearing, where were the smelling?

18 But now hath God set the members every one of them in the body, as it hath pleased him.

19 And if they were all one member, where were the body?

*20 But now are they many members, yet but **one body**.*

21 And the eye cannot say unto the hand, I have no need of thee: nor again the head to the feet, I have no need of you.

22 Nay, much more those members of the body, which seem to be more feeble, are necessary:

23 And those members of the body, which we think to be less honourable, upon these we bestow more abundant honour; and our uncomely parts have more abundant comeliness.

24 For our comely parts have no need: but God hath tempered the body together, having given more abundant honour to that part which lacked:

25 That there should be no schism in the body; but that the members should have the same care one for another.

26 And whether one member suffer, all the members suffer with it; or one member be honoured, all the members rejoice with it.

27 Now ye are the body of Christ, and members in particular.

28 And God hath set some in the church, first apostles, secondarily prophets, thirdly teachers, after that miracles, then gifts of healings, helps, governments, diversities of tongues.

29 Are all apostles? are all prophets? are all teachers? are all workers of miracles?

30 Have all the gifts of healing? do all speak with tongues? do all interpret?

31 But covet earnestly the best gifts: and yet shew I unto you a more excellent way.

God sees one body (believers) with many parts. Only when these parts are working together like a fine-tuned machine, will the body achieve the desired synergy. So why are the parts in rebellion? Why do people desire more meaningful roles? The church is divided more today than ever before. What would this world be like if those who followed Christ became truly "One Body" for him?

The inhabitants at Babel understood what it meant to work together for a common purpose. The Lord even commended them for that when he said;

> *6 And the LORD said, Behold, the people is one, and they have all one language; and this they begin to do: and now **nothing will be restrained from them**, which they have imagined to do.*

Nothing is impossible for mankind even today. We are unrestrained. The Lord did not come down and take the abilities, talents, and gifts away from them. Rather, He simply confused them so they would have to learn how to rely on one another all over again. They were humbled as their purpose was changed to one of simple survival. They would have to rely on each other for daily things. Their fears and anxieties would have been magnified. Their desires would have been focused on short-term areas like food or shelter. Somehow in all of this, I picture a loving god desperately trying to get the attention of each heart as if to say, "I am with you" or "I will give you your heart's desires."

WORLD PEACE?

A lthough there are people in this world who would like to wage war at all times, the majority still desire to live in peace. Yet, the question remains, "Is that possible?" Is there one definition to what peace on earth is, that everyone can adopt? Societies speak about it, but individuals tend to have unique views.

Remember the account in the Garden of Eden, where Adam and Eve were placed. They lived among the animals in perfect peace. I can picture Adam talking to the animals when each was given a name. There is no record of any beast going wild. They seemed to all eat the vegetation together. Imagine for a moment, dining with lions or petting a skunk. The original creation was one filled with peace. So what changed?

God's creation took on a oneness of their own. The gift of free choice was designed to allow man to choose to love and fellowship with the creator, but they could also choose to turn away. That was a risk that the creator needed to take. He didn't desire a world of human puppets, but rather one that mimicked the fellowship that was enjoyed in heaven. God knew that man would make some wrong choices, but that was something that had to occur if mankind was to truly love him back.

One of those choices came in the account of Adam's son Cain, who had a jealous spirit towards his brother Abel. That jealousy turned to rage and finally death. Cain couldn't hide from God, and when confronted, denied any wrongdoing. Prior to this event is the story of Adam and Eve's disobedience in eating from the forbidden tree. They also hid from God and tried to pass any blame onto someone else. To the creator these things are called sin and will permeate the lives of mankind for all generations to follow. Adam and Eve's disobedience caused them to be expelled from the garden. Peace would then be merely a dream. Man began to kill animals for food and clothing. Animals began to seek shelter. Man was now to be feared. Even the animals had to seek other animals for food as the lush vegetation was now lost.

Enemy of Unity

The story of the fall of man in the garden has been shared for ages. Adam and Eve were tempted by the serpent called Satan and gave in to his wiles. His methods were subtle and called upon man's desire to have significance. Until their fall, they did not know what bad was, only good. God was with them continuously. They made a choice to eat of the fruit of the Tree of Life, because it looked good and that they would be more like their creator. They were instructed by God not to eat of the fruit because they would understand about good/evil and surely die. They didn't know what those things were as they had not seen death, but they did desire to be more like God. Satan deceived and the unity they had in communion with God was lost. They now knew about evil.

Good and Evil: Gen2:16-17 (KJV)

16 And the LORD God commanded the man, saying, Of every tree of the garden thou mayest freely eat:

17 But of the tree of the knowledge of good and evil, thou shalt not eat of it: for in the day that thou eatest thereof thou shalt surely die.

Satan's Deception: Gen.3:5 (KJV)

5 For God doth know that in the day ye eat thereof, then your eyes shall be opened, and ye shall be as gods, knowing good and evil."

If there is one thing in this world that the Devil still desires today, it is to create disunity. This starts in the family home where couples are to be as one. Disobedience in children is a good thing to him. Societies that seek to put God first are his enemy. The best place to create division for Satan is to attack it from within. It is no wonder that we see areas like divorce, alcoholism, abortion, and other social patterns at all time highs, especially in America. The enemy is on a mission to destroy all that is good. When anyone reaches out to a loving God for help, Satan desires to take God's place. God is jealous god. Satan demands to be god on earth for mankind and the war continues until Jesus returns.

Spiritual Unity?

There are many people who seek a relationship with a higher source of strength, wisdom, or guidance than possible in human terms. Faith is a word that is used to describe that such a source exists. When people get to their ultimate bottom, emotionally, they cry "Oh God!" It seems to be preprogrammed in our being and is triggered by desperation. The teachings of Noah to his sons were passed on for the generations that followed. Somehow there was a breakdown and new generations would not hear about the love of a creator, His desire to meet our every need, and be our guide. This turning point in the lives of Ham's descendents might well have come from Noah's rebuke. As a father, I have had those times when my children needed correction, but I tried to make the punishment fit the incident. Ham was disrespectful when he made light of his drunkenness. Fathers are given tremendous responsibilities, as they are leaders in their families. Their leadership demands respect. Lack of respect demands consequences. But did the punishment fit the crime?

It would have been one thing if Noah made Ham perform extra duties or even serve his brothers for a season. It must have been something else when Noah cursed Caanan (Ham's son). When I first read that account, I was flabbergasted, as I thought that Caanan was an innocent victim. Now that I am a grandfather, the thought of condemning my grandchildren for anything my children did is beyond lunacy. Noah could have come to his senses and rectified the situation, but we have no account of that in scriptures. What we do see is Ham's descendents wandering the earth without Noah's faith in the creator that saved them in the flood. We read about the people of Babel who want to "build a name for themselves", because they are cursed as servants without the recognition of man.

Noah not only drank of the fruit of his vineyard, but he was found naked. Try to picture the scene. You come upon your father lying drunk on the ground. That scene, in and of itself, is not so unusual. Perhaps, you have seen the sight before. Now add to that the fact that he is lying naked. For me, that painted a totally different picture. It implied that there was more going on than just the results of stopping to drink of the vine and passing out. When the story was first read to me, I thought that both Ham and Noah were at fault. Noah didn't take responsibility for his actions. He only took revenge for Ham's. Somehow, I cannot help feel, that Noah caused Ham's generation to fall away as a direct result of his action (or lack of it). The account is there for us to learn a valuable lesson even today.

Gen.11:4 (NIV)

*4 And they said, Go to, let us build us a city and a tower, whose top may reach unto heaven; and **let us make us a name**, lest we be scattered abroad upon the face of the whole earth.*

Thousands of years have past since this account at Babel took place. Is that the end of the story? Perhaps the same lessons for man to learn are still present today. What were the motives of the people back then? Are there groups with similar motives around today? What will happen to them? If this account contains lessons for us today, then we need to examine these questions and others.

"…So that we can make a name (for ourselves)" speaks volumes about the human spirit and the need for identity. One of the best selling books of this century is "The Purpose Driven Life" by Rick Warren. In his book, Rick addresses the age old question, "Why am I here?" The search for the answer starts with the knowledge that God planned us from the very beginning. Rick describes the search for answers process as a "Spiritual Journey." When we know God's purpose for our lives, life will make sense. When we then choose to do the job that was made for us, our lives will achieve the highest rewards. When we approach the throne of God and hear the words, "Well done my child", we will rejoice.

The people at Babel wanted something else. For them the search was for recognition, namely self-righteousness. They wanted others to lift them up. They wanted a name that would instill awe in those who heard it. For them it was not a question of "Why we are here", but rather a statement that tells everyone "Who we are." They wanted people to identify them with greatness. They were not second-class citizens and had something to show the world. They had resolve and used it for a common purpose in building the city. God praised the resolve, but destroyed the purpose. Perhaps, God wanted them to find their true purpose.

History books are filled with people who desired to make a name for themselves, leading to destruction. Adolph Hitler filled a German nation with the false hope that their lives would be improved if they stood up against those who caused their demise. They had a common purpose, but it was not of God. Small countries like North Korea, and North Viet Nam desired to tell the world, they were bigger players.

September 11, 2001 will forever be etched in the minds of Americans as a well-planned group of terrorists made a statement of their own. Symbols of the American way of life became grave markers for over 3000 innocent people who lost their lives. Now a country is united for the common cause of defeating terror, along with the support of many other nations.

DENNIS A. MCINTYRE

21ˢᵀ CENTURY BABELS

Making a stand for something is not necessarily a bad thing. It is important to look at the motives behind it. God confused the language at Babel due to wrong motives and will take the appropriate action when similar motives are used today. Hitler was defeated by a coalition of countries who stood up, but not without many casualties. War may be necessary, but not the ultimate solution. Fifty years after North Korea surrendered in the Korean War, that same small country is flexing its muscles again with the threat of nuclear domination. Is divine intervention necessary once again?

Organizational Babels

Businesses

Businesses, school systems, political agendas, and religious institutions can be trying to create recognition that fails to honor the creator, especially in the United States. In business, we see top-level management seeking financial wealth at employee expense. Company stock soars because of false information and book keeping. Finally, the bubble bursts, the company is shattered, and people are looking for new dreams. Competition is considered a value for consumers who benefit from higher quality goods and services at reasonable costs. Consumers should be the driving force for corporations. Far too often we see this principle abused or ignored as corporate America uses political influences to gain high profits and reduced competition. Small companies with great products can no longer compete.

Business Babels are created when the quality of their offerings is overshadowed by greed or power. Examine the well known companies a decade ago and see how many are around today or in bankruptcy courts. What caused their demise? What could they have done differently? Now examine those that are growing. Where is their focus? Someone once said' "what goes around comes around". When companies continue to serve their employees and patrons with dignity and respect, positive results occur. When less positive motives are demonstrated a fall is eminent.

1. What would your business be like in ten years if the guiding principles aligned with the Creator's?

_____
_____
_____
_____

2. What differences would you expect to see in employees, customers, or the world?

_____
_____
_____
_____

School Systems

School systems are taking stands as well. I find it interesting that there has been more focus in the last decade than ever before to take God out of school. The Pledge of Allegiance was banned or altered because of the words "one nation under God". The right to worship as we please is being violated as students are banned from praying on school grounds. The case has been made, that it violates the rights of those who don't believe in God. The Ten Commandments have been displayed in public institutions from the days of our country's forefathers and now they are seen as infringements on religious rights.

America's institutions are quickly coming under judgment like the days of Sodom and Gomorrah. Satan is leading the revolution. The enemy is winning the battle, but victory will be the Lord's.

Political Agendas

What about politics in America? The 2004 election was staged with the remembrances of 2000 still heavy on the Democratic Party's heart. It was a significant loss and the tactics of the 2004 election tried to get voters to vote against the incumbent rather than for what the challenging party stood for. Although the vote was close, the heart of America voted their conscience. Geographically the country was united. The highly populated coastal areas were predominantly Democratic, while the less populated internal states voted with a different set of values and their candidate won. In a matter of speaking, the little people stood up.

America was founded primarily by individuals who understood that tyranny and oppression would not guide the land. These were things that they rebelled against in seeking their new found freedom as a country. Government was to be "of the people" and "for the people". To ensure this, each state would send delegates to the congress for short terms (typically one year). These delegates would sacrifice their responsibilities at home as a tour of duty. Their tasks were not taken lightly. Their states were given true representation.

Three distinct branches would be set up to create more equality, namely Judicial, Legislative, and Executive. The Legislative branch determined the laws (Constitution) . The Judicial branch interpreted according to the Constitution. The Executive branch carried out the duties prescribed in the laws. In all cases each branch embraced the basic "do unto others" principle.

The twenty-first century has significant differences from our forefathers. The idea of having several political parties started out as a good balance. Each would have differences that voters can align with based on their own needs and circumstances. Yet today this alignment is severely compromised. Parties are divided within themselves, leaving voters hard pressed to align with anyone. Ego clashes make the term "for the people" more like a remote dream. There is a strong move to change the judicial branch of government to no longer interpret the Constitution but to judge according to standards not within it. Big businesses and cities control the states, rather than represent them. Political representation today is a full time career rather than a tour of duty. People are being told what they need rather than being heard.

Religious Institutions

Then we have the religious institutions, which seem to be forming new divisions (sects) daily. Christian organizations top the list. Small differences in doctrine, like whether musical instruments are to be played in a service, create separation. It seems as though even followers of Christ desire to hang on to something they can claim as their own. Other issues like abortion, gay marriage, or outdated traditions, create separation. If Christians over the world could put the same energy used to divide the church, into uniting the cause of Christ, nothing would be impossible. This country was blessed because of the principles on which she was founded. Over ninety percent of those who signed the Declaration of Independence, confessed to being followers of Jesus Christ. Perhaps the terrorist attacks are America's wake up call.

Again, the words from Gen.11: 6 ring the bells of freedom in America:

> *6 And the LORD said, Behold, the people is one, and they have all one language; and this they begin to do: and now nothing will be restrained from them, which they have imagined to do.*

If as one religion, believers unite for the cause of Christ, then nothing they plan to do will be impossible for them. This was addressed to the people of Babel, but it has a future tense to it. In other words, if we align on the side of Christ once again, then our country can be spared from the fate given Sodom. That sounds pretty harsh, but we can examine the conditions going on in Sodom and how close we are to that today. Idols of money, lust, power, and greed permeate our societies. Divorce is at all time high levels. Substance abuse is at record levels. The list goes on.

History will always have its Babels, but unity for Christ will create significance for eternity. Treasures in heaven will not be destroyed.

LESSONS LEARNED

LESSON 1:
STRENGTH IN UNITY

4 Hour House

One of the desires of management in nearly all businesses is to develop teamwork. In sporting events we see athletes encouraging one another with high fives, arm pumps, and other gestures. It is an accepted fact that the strength of an organization comes from the unity within and not from a few individuals. In fact a few disgruntled workers can tear down organizations very quickly. Management has recognized the need to develop teamwork, trust, and respect in their workforce in order to achieve higher quality, efficiency, versatility, and customer satisfaction with their products. Automobile sales facilities have been working on this concept with everyone involved in sales and service to get customers to feel good about dealing with them. Corporations have used various tools and methods to unify groups like management or maintenance support.

One of these tools was presented to my engineering community. It was a video called, "The Four Hour House". I was very impressed and would recommend the video to any organization that desired unity. I was an electrical engineer at the time, but watched with engineers and technicians from other trades. Often mechanical engineers would start projects in my group and then later request electrical support to help them achieve their intended results. The movie showed that when these groups worked together from the beginning, better and more efficient designs could be achieved. In other words, the mechanical design may not turn out the way the mechanical engineer imagined. Better input from the electrical community up front may cause a design shift.

In the video two teams of people with varied skills were asked to design and build two separate houses (one house per team). They had no limit as to the number of people they could have, but they had the day of construction set as a focal point. Each team could have all the tools they would need, available, including any heavy equipment like cranes, hoists, or cement mixers. Raw materials would need to be specified (wood, cement, etc.) and they would be delivered to the site. Planning was essential or something would be lost. Unforeseen delays could severely handicap team performance. Therefore, everyone's input was needed continuously to avoid setbacks.

The lesson was simple. Anything is possible when people work as one for a common purpose. Insurmountable odds can be overcome. Great accomplishments are possible. Try to imagine an open piece of ground, with only a cement footing and piles of raw materials at eight A.M. Now imagine seeing people moving furniture into a completely finished home at that site before noon. Most people would say this is impossible. It was not only possible, it happened. The winning team completed their house in under four hours passing all inspections like electrical, plumbing, and etc.

Now imagine tasks like ending cancer, world hunger, or curing the common cold happening in your lifetime. The longer the timeframe, the more we might believe in the possibilities. In fact without such a belief the human spirit grows faint. Remember the Israelites leaving Egypt (Exodus) with the hope of a better life. As time passed so did their hope. They were even willing to go back to slavery.

LESSON 2:
NOTHING IS IMPOSSIBLE WITH GOD

This lesson speaks to everyone desiring a better life. School systems could be greatly improved if faculties could place all of their differences on the table, share improvement ideas, and collectively unite for the cause of producing young adults, who are more prepared to enter the world beyond. The opposite may be true when teachers or administrations, despite measurements indicating consistent declines in basic learning skills, protect curriculums. Pride says; "I have always done it that way." Empathy says; "Our students are falling short of the mark and WE need to find out why and make improvements." The same can be said for other organizations like businesses, hospitals, government bodies, and religious sects.

In the book of Revelation, John is given a vision and told to record it. The vision depicted the present as well as what was to happen in the future. Seven churches of that time received letters describing their deeds from God's perspective, each with unique differences, strengths, and shortcomings. These churches are symbolic of those today. Division among them was a problem that needed to be solved, but pride was a barrier. What if Christians in just one community put aside their differences and returned to the one first started in Acts, when people gathered in worship, shared food, and gave freely of themselves for the betterment of others?

(Rev.2: 1 – 7 **Ephesus**)… hard working, persevering, intolerant of evil, BUT "You have forsaken your first love."

(Rev.2: 8 – 11 **Smyrna**)… poverty yet rich, persecuted, encouraged to be faithful and receive eternal life.

(Rev. 2: 12 – 17 **Pergamum**)… faithful despite Satan's rule, BUT you are not rising up against false teachings.

(Rev. 2: 18 - 29 **Thyatira**)… growing church filled with love, faith, and good works, BUT tolerant of those teaching immoral behavior.

(Rev. 3: 1 – 6 **Sardis**)… outwardly alive, BUT inwardly dead. "Wake up."

(Rev. 3: 7 – 13 **Philadelphia**)… faithful yet weak, patiently enduring

(Rev. 3: 14 – 22 **Laodicea**)… neither hot nor cold, rich in worldly things yet poor, blind, and naked. (v16) "So, because you are lukewarm – neither hot nor cold – I am about to spit you out of my mouth."

Each church started out with a longing for the Lord. Many suffered persecution. Some were poor in worldly goods. Some turned from their faith. In every letter, however, each church is told that they can be right with God and receive eternal blessings if they overcome the world. To those of you who confess to be Christians, to what church do you belong? Are you lukewarm, which is detestable to God? Are you putting earthly values above eternal ones? United we can overcome the world.

The Spirit of God spoke to the churches of the first century. I believe the same spirit speaks to believers today with the same message of eternal hope if we persevere and remain true. That takes more than trying to be a good person. When people of faith unite, synergy occurs. Human beings seem to draw strength from each other as if they are not facing trials and tribulations alone. Survivors encourage Cancer patients. Others who endured similar losses comfort those who lose loved ones, especially at an early age. Often, I feel that God gives people trials to go through, so that sometime in the future they will encourage others, going through simlar trials.

God allows things to occur, but then works through hearts for another purpose. God cannot work through hardened hearts. Christians should have hearts that are open, producing faith, hope, and love to a needy world. Is Christ first in your life? If he were to return today, would he see your heart faithful and true? A united Christian community can change the world. Nothing is impossible with God. Jesus tells us that if we have only the faith of a mustard seed, we can move mountains (Matt. 17: 20 – 21). The inhabitants of Babel knew what it meant to work together in harmony. Just like then, we can accomplish far more for the kingdom of God united, than we can divided.

LESSON 3:
WE ARE HERE FOR A REASON

One of the best selling books of our time is called; "The Purpose Driven Life" by Rick Warren. In his book Rick describes insights to the basic human question: "Why am I here?" For the Christian, we are told that each of us have been given spiritual gifts along with talents, which should be used for advancing God's purposes. These gifts include areas like:

- **Speaking in tongues**
- **Encouragement**
- **Teaching**
- **Administration**
- **Interpretation**
- **Healing**
- **Prophesizing**
- **More**

These and more are listed in 1 Cor. 12. With such a wide variety of gifts, there must be a plan that allows all of our differences to work together for a common good. If our creator dispersed them, as he desired, then we must be able to use them collectively. 1 Cor. 12: 14 – 26 puts things in a different perspective. The body consists of arms, legs, hands, eyes, ears, and many more parts. Each one is significant. All parts should work together "(v24b – 25) so that there be no division in the body, but that its parts should have equal concern for each other."

When each of us find our true purpose in life, apply our god-given gifts, and share as one body in Christ, then the answer to the question "Why am I here?" will be clear. We again read about these gifts in the book of Ephesians.

Ephesians 4: 7 - 13 (KJV)

> *7 But unto every one of us is given grace according to the measure of the gift of Christ.*

> *8 Wherefore he saith, When he ascended up on high, he led captivity captive, and* **gave gifts unto men.**

> *9 (Now that he ascended, what is it but that he also descended first into the lower parts of the earth?*

> *10 He that descended is the same also that ascended up far above all heavens, that he might fill all things.)*

> *11 And he gave some, apostles; and some, prophets; and some, evangelists; and some, pastors and teachers;*

> *12 For the perfecting of the saints, for the work of the ministry, for the edifying of the body of* **Christ:**

> *13 Till we all come in the unity of the faith, and of the knowledge of the Son of God, unto a perfect man, unto the measure of the stature of the fullness of Christ:*

From Paul's words to the church at Ephesus we are given a picture of the risen Christ leaving some things for his creation in the form of grace and gifts along with the purpose behind them. We are to use them to build the body of Christ up. In doing so we can attain maturity in Christ. Believers and followers of Christ need to be united for him. Those things that divide Christians divide the body of Christ. He conquered death for us and asks us to conquer the world for him. This is certainly no small task, but we have been given the gifts and abilities to do the work.

...Paul continues with these words (Eph.4: 14 - 16 KJV):

14 That we henceforth be no more children, tossed to and fro, and carried about with every wind of doctrine, by the sleight of men, and cunning craftiness, whereby they lie in wait to deceive;

15 But speaking the truth in love, may grow up into him in all things, which is the head, even Christ:

16 From whom the whole body fitly joined together and compacted by that which every joint supplieth, according to the effectual working in the measure of every part, maketh increase of the body unto the edifying of itself in love.

We have a picture of the body with Christ as the head and from him every part is attached. From the various science classes that I have been taught, I understand that the head is where decisions and actions are handled. The body moves away from a hot stove when the brain sends commands down the spinal column to the arms and legs. Jesus referring to the grape vine, where we are the branches that rely on the vine for our growth, makes this same analogy.

Note: *Bruce Wilkinson offers wonderful insights into this in his book; "The Secrets of the Vine."*

Life on earth is but a blink compared to eternity. If we are placed here for one brief moment in time to accomplish a certain task with all the tools to do so, then we better figure out what that is in a hurry. We will either enter eternity with a strong welcome and sincere "Mission accomplished" or we will enter with words of sorrow from our creator.

The church at Laodicea was "neither hot nor cold" and God said he would "Spew them out of his mouth." In other words, we need to take a stand for something. Complacency is not a stand. Somehow societies have played the middle of the road song for some time. They seem to believe that if they leave everyone alone, they will be safe. Doctrines are altered, traditions are abandoned, and worst of all people begin to look the other way when unrighteousness infiltrates. Alcohol, drugs, and other agents become accepted if used in moderation. The institute of marriage clause; "till death do us part" is slowly changed with the added words; "unless it doesn't work out" leading to divorce. I do not believe we are placed here to "play the field" and test everything so that we will know what we want when we reach our eternal residence. If that were the case, why would each of us have unique gifts? Why would we be given specific rules of conduct if they were to be merely guidelines? Why do you think you are here?

LESSON 4:
COMMUNICATION IS THE KEY

The people of Babel had perfected the art of communication and were on the road to great accomplishments. The world would have looked upon the city and the tower with great admiration. The inhabitants would have embellished themselves with the accolades. Heads would have swelled with pride. Then what? Millionaires reaching one pinnacle of success often need new heights to challenge them. The challenge of new aspirations provides a level of new hope and pride. God surely knew that the tower would have been only the beginning for even more accomplishments for the people there. He also knew that life without him would be disastrous for everyone. Destroying the language kept them from new heights as well as shattered the present one. If these people applied the same energy building God's kingdom, nothing would be impossible for them.

In the very beginning the creator desired to communicate with his creation. I can picture regular one-on-one dialogs with Adam and God in the garden. I can picture Adam coming up with a name for an animal and then asking God what he thought of it. At some point God put Adam asleep and created a "helpmate" for him. Perhaps God sensed that Adam needed someone like himself to converse with on earth. Perhaps, Adam even asked for another being. Anyway, from that point on man began the process of human communication. The concept of words may have been a mystery as well. God could have given the pair a common speech or allowed Adam to teach Eve whatever language he knew.

Now our world has hundreds of languages, each one with dozens of unique dialects. Somehow we need to find ways to reach across the barrier of words and reestablish ways to communicate with one another. One language transcends all languages, namely the language of love. Words do not have to be spoken to have love felt. A bowl of soup given to someone hungry or a blanket to another shivering in the cold speaks this language. The idea that we have many languages today is not the problem, but the challenge. Somehow we need to speak a more universal language. Once spoken hearts will be changed and hope will be restored.

Communication was there in the beginning, even before the earth was formed. We are told several times in Genesis chapter 1, that "God said" and it was so. Creation was the result of an all knowing, all powerful creator simply speaking the words and they became real. Everything was created in this way until man came along.

Gen.1:26 – 27 (KJV):

26 And God said, Let us make man in our image, after our likeness: and let them have dominion over the fish of the sea, and over the fowl of the air, and over the cattle, and over all the earth, and over every creeping thing that creepeth upon the earth.

*27 So God created man in his **own image**, in the image of God created he him; male and female created he them.*

Who is God speaking to? "Let US" is plural. There had to be more than one prior to creation. We don't see the words "MY image" or "MY likeness". Creation was the result of a committee in heaven communicating with each other and then coming to a decision to create the world. Then we need to understand why man would be different than all the other living things. We were created in their image and likeness. Each member present during creation had a voice. Then verse 27 says that God created us in HIS image. It all may sound confusing until we recognize that the committee in heaven was God in all forms.

We pour water, hold ice cubes, and hear steam whistling from a teakettle, yet each are one in the same. Water can take the forms of a liquid, a solid, or a gas. We don't seem to have a problem with that, but when it comes to God, whom we can't see, touch, or feel, then we do. I believe that God the Father, God the Son, and God the Spirit are all different parts of the same God. The Father can be likened to our earthly father who helped give us life. God the Son came as a man to live with us, learn from us, and even die for us. We may not see him, but we can surely know him. Then at Pentecost after Jesus had gone, the promise of a Holy Spirit being sent to mankind was fulfilled. The spirit can indwell in us as a teacher and friend. Three forms, but one God, each with a purpose. To be singled out from all creation is something special indeed. Unlike the water-ice-steam illustration, God is all forms at the same time, since time is something mankind measures. God was there in the beginning, is in the present, and knows the future.

Communication is also what God desires from us. He wants man to talk to him daily. Why else would he make us in his image? Why else would he create the world and place us here? Why else would he send his son to die so that we can be with him for all eternity?

Suppose I had a treasure map, cut it into many pieces, and then distributed the pieces to every person I saw. Then I told them that they all could share in the treasure but first they needed to locate it. They would need to find a way to get the map back together, study it, and collectively follow it to the treasure. If Christians have the pieces, but don't communicate the treasure is forever lost. We have been given the pieces to unite people everywhere. We need to seek the treasure.

LESSON 5:
WE NEED TO PASS THE BATON

The 4 x 100 relay race involves various runners passing a baton after completing their segment. A poor pass often means they will lose the race. A dropped pass means for them the race is over. We only need to look at events in history, that show how the teachings of one generation can easily get lost in others to follow when they are not properly passed.

Noah must have faithfully passed on what he knew about God to his sons while in the ark. They went their separate ways, yet for generations they maintained the same language and dialect. I believe the account of Noah found naked and drunk by Ham is a huge lesson for each of us today. The descendents of Ham seemed to lose their way. The tower at Babel indicated that that desired a name for themselves and to not be scattered again. Somehow, the name of God was not mentioned. Somehow, they felt as if they lost their family roots.

What are the values that you are passing on to your children?

_____

_____

_____

_____

When have you picked up a paper and seen the front page filled with good news? For some reason media coverage of events tends to focus on negative events. Good things don't sell. It is as if people want to see how bad the rest of the world is in order to justify something good about their own world. Ham's descendents at Babel took a stand desiring a better life. Their history was filled with bad news. Home was a dream before their arrival. Family ties had been severed. They were going to do something to get noticed. Perhaps, what they were attempting to build would have made the front page of their time.

Ham was disrespectful to his father. Children rebel as part of their learning process. How we handle the rebellion as parents can make all the difference in how they turn out in the future. Although we might desire perfection in our children, we should not expect it as the norm. We can only theorize what Noah may have felt before passing judgment on Ham and his son, Caanan. His reaction came after he awoke from his drunkenness, which may have lacked good judgment of his own. Perhaps, he still wasn't thinking straight and the disrespect amplified his feelings. We may consider anger in Noah's voice.. Nevertheless, his action was final and we have no indication that he ever withdrew the curse.

Sometimes our children cause us to react quickly and inflict harsh punishment without taking the time to gather our thoughts. Later we feel remorse and go back to help make amends. Seeking forgiveness from our children makes us swallow our pride and recognize that we were wrong as well. Punishment out of anger can teach children to fear more than to feel ashamed of their own actions.

Our father in heaven wants us to feel love and learn from our mistakes. Imagine what Ham must have felt after his own father revoked blessings and condemned his son to a life of servant hood. I can't imagine any feelings of fatherly love. Feelings of abandonment, anger, doubt, guilt, loneliness, and low self worth may well have been felt. The place where he may have felt loved and needed would have been lost.

I lost my mother when I was three years of age to cancer. Although I didn't know her, feelings of abandonment have been with me through adulthood. Several years of abusive relationships in foster homes caused a wee small voice to cry out inside; "Doesn't anybody love me?" As a father I would never want my children to have these feelings. The legacy that I would desire to leave must include the knowledge that I may not like the behavior, but I will always love my family. The account in Genesis 10 seems out of place in the lineage of Noah at first glance. When we take a second look, perhaps we see a lesson for us even today. Others are watching our words, actions, mannerisms, and values, especially those we are closest to.

Our legacy needs to be filled with love, encouragement, and good will to produce similar qualities in our children. These same qualities are needed in all relationships as they build joy, self worth, and other positive attributes in those around them.

The lowest shared unit in society is the family. It can be the weakest link when discontent exists or the strongest when love abounds. Children who feel loved and accepted are less likely to succumb to less desirable outside influences. Those who doubt are more likely to seek contentment from others. There are those in leadership that believe it takes more than a family to raise a child. These people look at the picture from the top down. They see a hurt and put a bandage on it. They don't address the cause of the hurt, which requires looking at the situation from the bottom up. Outward healing may appear, yet feelings of rejection, low self-esteem, fear, or abandonment may remain. If the root problem is not addressed, then bigger band-aids will be needed in the future. It takes a family to raise a child and provide the groundwork for future growth. That is the legacy our children need.

Our faith in an all-knowing and loving God is our baton and we need to pass it on.

LESSON 6:
GOD IS PATIENT WITH US

Genesis 9:28 (KJV)

28 And Noah lived after the flood three hundred and fifty years.

Noah died at the age of 950 years. He was 600 when the flood came. His sons were with him for a time following the flood and then they scattered to replenish the earth. Noah had time to think about his actions towards Ham. Reports from his offspring from distant parts may have been received, but we can only speculate. I can only imagine what reactions Noah might have had from each report. How might he have handled learning of the wickedness of Sodom and Gomorrah? One thing is certain. God is patient with his creation.

Sodom and Gomorrah were so wicked that not even ten righteous people could be found there and he finally destroyed them with fire. God sent Jonah to Nineveh to warn them of their wickedness. They repented and were spared.

Jonah 3 (KJV) Jonah Goes to Nineveh

1 And the word of the LORD came unto Jonah the second time, saying,

2 Arise, go unto Nineveh, that great city, and preach unto it the preaching that I bid thee.

3 So Jonah arose, and went unto Nineveh, according to the word of the LORD. Now Nineveh was an exceeding great city of three days' journey.

4 And Jonah began to enter into the city a day's journey, and he cried, and said, Yet forty days, and Nineveh shall be overthrown.

5 So the people of Nineveh believed God, and proclaimed a fast, and put on sackcloth, from the greatest of them even to the least of them.

6 For word came unto the king of Nineveh, and he arose from his throne, and he laid his robe from him, and covered him with sackcloth, and sat in ashes.

7 And he caused it to be proclaimed and published through Nineveh by the decree of the king and his nobles, saying, Let neither man nor beast, herd nor flock, taste any thing: let them not feed, nor drink water:

8 But let man and beast be covered with sackcloth, and cry mightily unto God: yea, let them turn every one from his evil way, and from the violence that is in their hands.

9 Who can tell if God will turn and repent, and turn away from his fierce anger, that we perish not?

10 And God saw their works, that they turned from their evil way; and God repented of the evil, that he had said that he would do unto them; and he did it not compassion and did not bring upon them the destruction he had threatened.

Here we see the city at Nineveh was not destroyed by the Lord. The people were allowed to start over again. God is patient with them as he is with us today. After the loss of his wife, my father was bitter against the God he was raised to believe in. My mother had converted from her Jewish background only a short time before learning of her cancer and now she was gone. How could God take her and leave three boys at a time when everything was going so well may have been his thought. For fifty years dad turned from the Lord, but the Lord never left him. At 89, with everything gone that was used as a replacement for God; dad repented and was reunited again. The first words he spoke afterwards, when I asked him who he would see in heaven, he answered "Your mother." I thank God that he is faithful and patient with us.

LESSON 7:
OUR HOPE IS WITH GOD NOT MAN

God spared Noah and his family from the destruction of the flood, because he was a righteous man. Perhaps we are being reminded that even the best still have human weaknesses and will fail at times. Noah was a man right with God, but still subject to moments of weakness. As much as we may love another human being, they will fail us. Some will demonstrate in word or action something that offends us. Others leave without notice and we never hear from them again. We will not live on earth forever and that will cause voids in the lives left behind. God tells us he will never leave us or forsake us. He is eternal. He is faithful. He is true to his word. He is our hope.

Religious leaders create false hopes in many sects. People have been known to sell everything they own, give the money to the organization, and then follow with a reverence that seems to approach some form of hypnotism. Many have been told of a specific day when the Lord will return and lose everything when the day passes. What is it in man that desires hope beyond this life? Why are we so willing to cling to something or someone for a brighter tomorrow?

Somehow we have a drive for something beyond human existence. Animals are content with what they have. Man is searching for something more. The people at Babel created hope in a new life. They drew strength from each other. The faith they had was in their own ability to make a difference. The Lord saw them with a unified purpose that left him out. How often do we try to accomplish something on our own merit? Our cry for help comes as a last resort, when all our efforts fail.

Chastisement from a parent can leave us feeling lost and abandoned. We may recognize our mistakes and seek to restore the severed relationship. When we feel loved again our hope is restored. When we don't feel loved, we feel worse. Children of broken relationships often take responsibility as if they caused the problem. The hope young newlyweds have on their wedding day may quickly wane in disillusionment. Whatever the situation, we need to know that we can place our hope in someone who will never fail us. Although we fail, he will still be by our side. He is ready, willing, and able to pull us out of any despair. He is our creator and desires to be Lord of our lives. He stands knocking on our heart waiting for us to open the door.

God changed the people of Babel by breaking their unity, but he wanted them to unite with him. They needed to find a home filled with joy, peace, and love. They were scattered again without hope. What a sad commentary, when God was only a prayer away.

LESSON 8:
NONE OF US ARE PERFECT

God does not desire perfection in us in order to carry out his purposes. He does require our faith. No one is or has ever been perfect except Jesus. Our humanity has been infected with the disease of sin since the fall of Adam and Eve. Romans 5:8 says:

"...while we were still sinners, Christ died for us."

Again in Romans 3:23 we read:

"for all have sinned and fall short of the glory of God".

Despite our imperfections God looks at our heart. He used David to conquer the giant, Goliath, knowing that he would later commit adultery with Bathsheba and have her husband (Uriah) placed at the front line of battle to be killed. David's psalms show a heart of remorse. Through his lineage God presented Jesus to the world.

Perfection is not possible on earth for mankind. We can strive for it by seeking to be like Jesus, who set the example. As long as we live we are subject to free choices, Satan's temptations, and the other worldly interventions. Yet, Jesus desires for us to join him in a perfect place for all eternity. It sounds like a dilemma. We read these words in Romans 6:23:

"For the wages of sin is death, but the gift of God is eternal life"

From the creation of the world and everything in it, God knew man would fall short, but the gift of free will was necessary. He didn't desire robots for communion. Can you picture the child, who did something wrong, and then freely came to a parent to say they were sorry? If that parent was you, how would that make you feel? Now magnify that feeling with God when even one sinner turns to him with a repentant heart. Our gifts and talents become God's tools when our heart is drawn to him.

Consider Paul, whose zealousness to protect the Jewish Law set out to stop the new movement called Christianity. The Lord met him on the road to Damascas (Acts 9) and said:

4 Saul, Saul, why persecutest thou me?

Saul was a Pharisee dedicated to uphold the written laws handed down over generations to the Jewish nation. He was very learned in the Old Testament writings and made it his life's work to protect them. Jesus met him as the very object of those writings. Later Saul would be called Paul and become, perhaps, the greatest supporter of Christianity. God used Paul and his abilities to further his cause and uses us today if we are willing. Paul's knowledge of the old prophesies was used to demonstrate that Jesus had fulfilled them. Paul no longer had to protect the law since it was made new again in Jesus.

Moses was hardly a great orator. Yet, God called him to lead a nation from bondage. In the process Moses killed an Egyptian. Moses was not perfect. Jonah rejected God's call and a big fish was sent to change his mind. Because of his words, the city of Nineveh was spared, yet, Jonah sulked. Jonah was not perfect yet God used him.

In the account at Babel we see how Noah's actions affected generations to follow. God used him to save mankind's existence from a flood, but still Noah was just a man. He was seen as righteous and faithful. The building of an ark demonstrated his desire to heed the calling despite enormous ridiculing from those who saw him. Faithfulness is an admirable trait that is becoming extinct. Marriages seem to fail far too often from infidelity (unfaithfulness). Noah reacted to Ham's ridiculing and disrespect with a harsh condemnation that may have led to the rebellion at Babel.

Noah was both naked and drunk. Some writers believe that Caanan (Ham's son) played a part in Noah's demise and that is why he was cursed. That idea sounds more like a justification for Noah's actions and is without evidence to substantiate. We know that Noah was a righteous man as God spared him and his family from the flood. Nevertheless he was still a man. His actions were his own regardless of the circumstances. At this point we can only speculate. Perhaps his reactions were the result of pride; after all he earned respect not ridicule.

One thing that we do not read is that he felt bad about his decision to curse Caanan. There is no indication that he sought for an apology. His decision was final even towards his own grandson. As a father I am guilty of punishing my children hastily, but I also felt led to seek forgiveness from my children later after some soul-searching. When fathers invoke punishment on their children it is meant to also teach them. What was the lesson that Ham learned? The account at Babel indicates that his descendents felt abandoned.

The lesson we can learn from this is that even though we will make mistakes, God can still use us for a greater purpose if we let him be our heavenly father. The descendents of Ham could have turned to God for their strength no matter what else happens, yet they choose to "make a name for themselves". In their minds the god of their father (Noah) abandoned them when they were cut off from their earthly family. The tower was not completed. Their communication was severed. Yet God did not abandon them.

Noah appears to react hastily to the ridicule of his son and Ham's descendents paid the price. Our actions often affect others. Abraham lied to the Pharaoh of Egypt about Sarah being his sister rather than his wife out of fear (Gen. 12: 10 – 20). God sent serious diseases on Pharaoh and his household as a result. Abraham lied and the Egyptians paid the price. Then Abraham was given great wealth. How unfair. Abraham entered Egypt due to a famine. In Gen.26: 1 – 10 his son Isaac would repeat the same lie concerning Rebekah to the king of the Philistines. Again the situation involved a famine. God used imperfect people despite their shortcomings and blessed them. Abraham would prove his faithfulness by offering Isaac as a sacrifice and then become the father of the nation of Israel. Isaac would be included in the lineage of Jesus (Matt. 1).

God knows we will fail. Only God is perfect. Although our failures deserve punishment, God uses them to build character. Abraham, Isaac, David and many others learned to seek God to help them overcome their failures. God sees each heart and pours out abundant mercy to those who love him. The imperfect are made perfect. Paul says it well in Phil. 4:13:

"I can do all things through Christ which strengtheneth me."

Note:

King James uses the word "which" and not "who" as interpreted by most other versions. I believe that the Holy Spirit of God lives inside a believer, who has accepted Christ as Savior and Lord. Allowing the spirit to work within me provides peace, joy, and much more. The very act of doing things for Christ through the spirit is my strength.

Lesson 9:
Learn From the Past

Noah didn't have the luxury of the internet, extensive libraries, or other media available in our modern era. Perhaps, he had some information from anchient manuscripts, but history can teach us about what works or fails over time. We all make mistakes. The key is to learn from them. Chastizing Caanan for his father's actions had several adverse affects.

First, we see the loss of family unity. Fathers are the head of the family unit. After Ham left with his family, ties with his father were broken. Parents and grandparents offer wisdom for their children and grandchildren. Unless Ham does a turn around, that wisdom is lost forever. It is certainly not going to be gained from new acquaintances in foreign lands with a different history. Idol worship and other traditions are a sharp contrast to following one God. Ham's descendants were raised in such a culture.

Second, family values can be altered. Noah held true to the God that he followed in building the ark. Ham must have known all too well about a righteous God. Imagine a hundred years of work, forty days of rain, and months inside the ark before touching land. He had time to fully understand that God was in control of everything. After the flood, the process of re-population began, with everyone doing their roles. Until his father's curse, Ham held true to those values. Now he had to be the leader for his family as they began to wander. The vineyards of his father were no longer a source for food as they traveled. He had no land to plant, nor the time to wait for its fruits. Living off the land took on new meaning. New values would be made with a new lifestyle. Ham knew how to work hard working the soil, but now the soil was no longer available.

Third, spiritual growth can be disrupted. Noah was the spiritual leader. Ham would have needed to cling to all that his father had taught him and take the same leadership roll for his family. Severing ties with his father might also sever feelings of respect. The story continues with strong negative spiritual results. Ham's descendents pass through some of the worst recorded cities in the Bible. Sodom and Gomorrah were totally destroyed due to their wickedness. Nineveh was spared only when they repented.

Nimrod became a mighty warrior and led the effort to build the tower at Babel. The only faith recorded at that time was in their own desires. They were not following the God of Noah, but rather their collective powers. Together, they were going to make a name for themselves. Together, they were going to earn respect. Unlike Noah, who relied on God, these people only relied on themselves.

History teaches us what works and what doesn't. It was recorded that Edison tried hundreds of combinations in creating the light bulb. He learned from each failure, but persevered until one prevailed. The founding fathers of America knew that if they were to survive and establish a new government, tyrany needed to be replaced with "of the people" rule. They also desired that individual freedoms needed to be protected. They further understood, that faith had brought them across the sea and led them to their independence from England. Tremendous unity led them to the government system that we have today.

Unfortunately, new generations have not learned from history. America has been the envy of the world. Freedom from oppression brought many through her borders, along with other freedoms like religion and speech. Over ninety percent of her founders cited their Christian faith as the controlling reason for America's growth. The insurmountable odds of crossing thousands of miles across a raging ocean and then to win freedom from a dominant foe are examples of God's intervention.

These founders felt the need to include biblical principles in their governing documents. Terms like "Under God" and "In God We Trust" were used extensively. Children learned to read and write with the Bible as a textbook. The Ten Commandments were displayed with pride as basic rules for conduct. They knew that all that was accomplished in bringing the colonies together as a nation was the direct result of a loving God's protection and direction.

For over two hundred years, America held true to these values. The gods of other sects were welcomed into her borders along with different cultures and languages. Slowly, the foundational soil has eroded. Devout athiests added fuel to the fire by saying that the word "god" was offensive to them and their freedom of religion. They fought to have it removed. History has shown one thing is certain when it comes to the fall of nations. That is that the best way to destroy a nation is from within. America has been infiltrated with Trojan horses for many years.

The Ten Commandments have been removed from government buildings. That is paramount to condoning murder, coveting, stealing, etc. The supreme court ruled that the first three commandments were offensive to other religions.

1. You shall have no other gods before me.
2. You shall make no idols
3. You shall not take the name of the Lord your God in vain.
4. You shall not murder.
5. You shall not commit adultery.
6. You shall not steal
7. You shall not bear false witness against your neighbor.
8. You shall not covet.
9. Keep the Sabbath day holy
10. Honor your father and mother

Bibles and other books that referenced God were banned from government mandated school systems (public schools). The pledge of allegiance was removed from public display because of the words "Under God." The list goes on and on. Now let's look at the effects in history.

First, the last decades have shown a tremendous increase in school violence, Mass shootings seem to be more common than ever before, Illegal drugs are poisoning the minds of children with generations following gods like money, power, and prestige. Divorce rates are escalating.

Second, The principles that guided the founding fathers proved to be good as America grew. The last decades have her in a state of bondage with tens of trillions of dollars in debt to foreign countries. Decay from within has begun. The events of September 11, 2001 did reveal that the heart of the country still fights tyranny, but that fight has a bigger foe. If the God of the Bible is real and being removed or replaced by idols of money or power, then it would make sense that His protection would be removed as well. If God is real, then Satan has a foothold. On the other hand, if God is not real, then what can account for the tremendous growth and prosperity of this nation over the past centuries? I leave that question for my readers.

Third, the Bible is still the number one best selling book in the world. Efforts to stop its production have failed. If God does not exist, then why have these efforts been unsuccessful. The name of God may have been removed from government buildings and schools, but not his diety. The Bible is His written word and a road map for human behavior. It has stood the test of time.

Mark 13: 31 tells us:

Heaven and earth shall pass away: but my words shall not pass away.

It is a history lesson for the world as well as a warning for the future. Jesus' disciples asked about when future destruction would occur in Mark13:4-10.

4 Tell us, when shall these things be? And what shall be the sign when all thee things shall be fullfilled?

5 And Jesus answering them began to say, Take heed lest any man deceive you:

6 For many shall come in my name, saying, I am Christ; and shall deceive many.

7 And when ye shall hear of wars and rumours wars, be ye not troubled: for such things must needs be; but the end shall not be yet.

8 For nation shall rise against nation, and kingdom against kingdom: and there shall be earthquakes in divers places, and there shall be famines and troubles: these are the beginnings of sorrows.

9 But take heed to yourselves: for they shall deliver you up to councils; and in the synagogues ye shall be beaten: and you shall be brought before rulers and kings for my sake, for a testimony against them.

10 And the gospel must first be published among all nations.

Although these disciples understood that Jesus was speaking about the fall of their temple and nation, His words applied to all nations. Scholars have tried to prove God's word is flawed without success. Modern media has recorded an increase in wars, earthquakes, famines, and other events. Global warming has a strong following as well. The word "god" may be removed from public view, but man cannot take God out of the world. That's His choice alone. I pray that doesn't happen.